Copyright © 2016 by Rabbi Avraham Katz

All rights reserved. This book or any portion thereof may not be reproduced or used in any manner whatsoever without the express written permission of the publisher except for the use of brief quotations in a book review.

Printed in the United States of America

First Printing, 2016

ISBN: 978-0-9974010-0-4

Editing: Rabbi Yehuda Altein
Layout and cover design: Yosef Yitzchok Turner
Distribution: Seforimdeals.com
Printed by The Print House

Please send comments to avraham.t.katz@gmail.com

TABLE OF CONTENTS

Recommendations v
Preface vii
How to Use This *Sefer* 1
General Introduction 7

SECTION 1:
  BASIC DAVENING 15
Chapter 1.
  Requesting and Thanking Hashem for Our Needs 17
Chapter 2.
  Thinking About Hashem Throughout the Day 21

SECTION 2:
  PIRUSH HAMILOS 23
Chapter 1.
  Concentrating on the *Pirush Hamilos* of the Set *Tefilos* 25
Chapter 2.
  How to Develop *Kavanah* 33
Chapter 3.
  Synchronizing the *Kavanah* With the Words 39
Chapter 4.
  Preparing for Davening and Staying Focused 43
Chapter 5.
  Kavanah When Saying Hashem's Names and the First *Possuk* of *Shema* 51
Chapter 6.
  Kavanos When Performing Mitzvos 57
Chapter 7.
  The *Chassidishe Pirush Hamilos* 63

SECTION 3:
  THINKING CHASSIDUS 65
Chapter 1.
  Transforming One's Perspective 69

| III

Chapter 2.
    Searching for *Elokus* 83
Chapter 3.
    To Be Real 85
Chapter 4.
    Ultimate Joy 89
Chapter 5.
    Profound and Practical 93
Chapter 6.
    Learning and Thinking Chassidus 97
Chapter 7.
    Real *Hisbonenus* 111
Chapter 8.
    Putting Effort Into Thinking Chassidus 115
Chapter 9.
    Enjoying Chassidus 121

SECTION 4:
    CHESHBON HANEFESH 125
Introduction 127
Chapter 1.
    Knowing Who We Are and Where We Are Going 129
Chapter 2.
    Making a *Seder* 133
Chapter 3.
    Making a *Cheshbon Hanefesh* 137
Chapter 4.
    Making *Hachlatos* 141
Chapter 5.
    Writing a *Duch* 145
Chapter 6.
    Teshuvah 147
Chapter 7.
    The Proper Approach to Making a *Cheshbon Tzedek* 151
Chapter 8.
    Thinking Chassidus before Going to Sleep 157

RECOMMENDATIONS

Rabbi Dr. Yaakov Brawer
Renowned expert on Chassidic thought

The ever-increasing complexity of the challenges facing Jews in our rapidly changing world has taken a toll on our commitment to authentic Chassidus in general and to *avodah* in particular. The damage is exemplified by an oxymoron in common usage: *"davening b'avodah."* This expression implies that there is a davening without *avodah*, which, moreover, is perceived by many as the norm.

Prayer is defined as *avodah shebalev*. *Avodah* is and has always been the heart of Chassidus Chabad, a fact of which we seem to be losing sight.

Much of the problem is due to the lack of knowledge on the practical level. Although most are familiar with the classical Chassidic sources on *avodah*, we do not know how to implement their teachings in our daily prayer.

A Practical Guide to Davening by Rabbi Avraham Katz goes a long way to addressing this problem. This highly original, clearly written text guides the reader in the acquisition of the practical skills essential to meaningful prayer. The author combines insight into human nature, educational expertise and a comprehensive grasp of Chassidus to produce an interesting, user-friendly compendium appropriate for everyone. The value of this book is inestimable.

Rabbi Yossi Paltiel
Mashpia in Chovevei Torah and Machon Chana
and popular teacher and mentor

I have always felt strange about writing *haskamos* for *sefarim*. I find it hard to imagine that every person who has endorsed a *sefer* has read enough of it to be qualified to endorse it, and frankly I'm in awe of people who can do that.

In this case, however, I am not endorsing the *sefer*, but I do want to say something about the author. Although endorsing a person entails a far greater responsibility than endorsing what he has written, for me at least this is more real.

Rabbi Avraham Katz is a real Yid, an *eved Hashem*. Davening and connecting to his Creator are serious and real for him. Accordingly, this *sefer* is not merely a reflection of someone who did research on a topic. In effect, it is a record of his journey and experience trying to connect to his Maker.

As a consequence, the credibility of the material herein is real because it has the third dimension, the investment of an individual for whom this journey is the story of his own personal life.

I trust that many people will find this *sefer* of interest and be motivated to make a similar journey based on what Rabbi Avraham Katz has lived and recorded.

PREFACE

With thanks and gratitude to Hashem, I present before Temimim and Anash the present *sefer*, *A Practical Guide to Davening*.

A Practical Guide to Davening is a collection of guidance and practical advice on how to make a *seder avodah* in davening—an organized, well thought-out plan that will allow davening to produce the tremendous positive affect it can potentially have on us.

There are four main goals this *sefer* strives to achieve:

1. To present a complete picture of what goes into real davening. The experience of davening is built on all of its many components—sincerity, focusing on the meaning of the words, being aware of Hashem's presence, and demanding of ourselves to act upon our connection with Him. When davening as a whole is seen in this light, it is much easier to appreciate what it is really all about.

2. To explain how to make a detailed plan to develop the ability to focus and concentrate during davening. Having such a plan is crucial. Let's say you have decided to begin having *kavanah* during davening. If you say to yourself that you will have *kavanah* during the entire davening every day, it's quite obvious you won't be able to accomplish your goal. But if you will make an organized plan how to develop your concen-

tration, you will actually succeed in having *kavanah* during davening and reap the benefits of doing so.

3. To explain how to develop the ability to be *misbonen*. *Hisbonenus* means to reflect upon an idea thoroughly, so that the subject matter will become fully internalized over the course of time, thereby having a tremendous impact on one's outlook and life. This practice is fundamental to Chabad Chassidus; however, it is impossible to attain without proper development.

4. To explain how to carry out a proper *cheshbon hanefesh*. To carry out a proper *cheshbon hanefesh* means to reflect upon who I am, what my purpose is, and what I should do to accomplish my purpose. When done properly and followed by real *hachlatos*, this process leads a person on the path of true *avodah*, giving him the aility to work on himself and fulfill his mission in life.

In all the above, the booklet illustrates how one can start from the most basic level of davening and work upwards, until he can reach more advanced levels of davening. This *sefer* is geared for anyone at any level, enabling him to see from where he should start and how he can advance.

This *sefer* also strives to give an idea of the way the Rebbe taught us to daven. It is of vital importance to every Chossid that every part of Yiddishkeit be permeated with the Rebbe's outlook on it; how much more so is this the case with regard to davening, the backbone of Yiddishkeit.

* * *

Many of the ideas presented in this booklet might not be new for the average davener. Nonetheless, this *sefer* can assist in clarifying from where one should start and how one should continue. It used to be more common for a *bochur* to approach his *mashpia* and ask him for a *seder avodah*, and he would thus know what to do and how to daven. Unfortunately, there are many who don't even know what to ask because they never saw great Chassidim davening, saying *Krias Shema Al Hamitah*, or being *misbonen* in a topic of Chassidus. Many people don't know what to ask and where to start, and this *sefer* can help them gain the clarity they are looking for.

Additionally, this *sefer* can contribute to those who do know what to ask as well. By reminding ourselves what real davening is all about and how important it is in our lives, we will come to do more and care more about davening.

The collection of advice is primarily taken from Shulchan Aruch and Chassidus, and especially from the *sichos*, *maamorim*, and *igros* of the Rebbe (and Frierdiker Rebbe). It also incorporates advice I received from various *mashpi'im*, primarily from R. Yitzchok Meir Gurary, the *mashpia* in Tomchei Temimim of Montreal for over 50 years,[1] as well as my own limited experience in attempting to daven properly.

I would like to thank my *mashpia* R. Yitzchok Meir Gurary for the *hadrachah* incorporated into this *sefer*, and the numerous individuals whose comments and feedback assisted in the creation and development of the ideas presented here.

In particular I would like to thank my editor, R. Yehuda Altein, for the tremendous work he put into helping this *sefer* become a reality, and for making the content of this *sefer* easy

---

1. Much of what went into this *sefer* is based on (my understanding of) his advice, and his encouragement was of great assistance; however, he did not personally go through the booklet in detail to check for accuracy. Any error or inaccuracy is entirely the author's.

to understand and apply. May he and his family be blessed with all good things, and may he continue to go from strength to strength.

My thanks to Rabbi Sholom Dovber Avtzon (author of the Rebbeim Biography series and Early Chassidic Personalities series) for his encouragement and advice towards the publishing of this *sefer*. May he be blessed with continued success in all his endeavors.

I would also like to thank Rabbi Yaakov Gershon for his scholarly assistance; Yoram Henquin for his assistance in the early stages of the *sefer*; Yosef Yitzchok Turner for the layout and cover design; and Shlomo Leib Goldman (administrator at seforimdeals.com) for distributing the *sefer*.

I am grateful to all those who provided me with feedback during the development of the *sefer*, helping develop many points and ideas.

This project would not have been possible without the constant support of my wife, Chaya Miriam. May Hashem bless her with true *chassidishe nachas*, continued health, and *menuchah*.

I would also like to thank the many individuals whose financial support enabled me to undertake the costs of editing and printing this *sefer*. May Hashem *bentch* each one of you in whatever you need, *mitoch harchavah*.

* * *

This *sefer* is intended to be the first of a three-part series on davening, with Hashem's help.

The author is in the process of preparing the second *sefer* in the series, a *likut* of various letters, *yechidusin*, and *sichos* from the Rebbe and the Frierdiker Rebbe containing practical advice relating to davening, *hisbonenus*, and *Krias Shema Al Hamitah*.

While the present *sefer* strives to explain the various components of davening and give a whole picture of what goes into real davening, it does not discuss specific ideas and topics that should be thought through during davening. This is an entire topic for itself that requires its own *sefer*, the third *sefer* in the series, which the author plans on preparing with Hashem's help.

* * *

I hope and pray that this pamphlet will result in renewed awareness of and excitement in davening to its readers. May it be Hashem's will that our minds and hearts will be opened to understanding and applying the teachings of Chassidus in our lives with joy and gladness of heart, *bekarov mamosh!*

Avraham Katz

Purim Katan (14 Adar Rishon), 5776
24 years from when the Rebbe gave out the *maamar Ve'atah Tetzaveh*[2]

---

2. This *maamar* was personally handed out by the Rebbe to men, women, and children in honor of Purim Katan, 5752, and as of now it is the last *maamar* we were privileged to receive from him.

    This *maamar* describes how the Rebbe empowers each and every one of us to internalize our faith in Hashem. This is accomplished through our own efforts at working on ourselves and awakening our love of and dedication to Hashem from the depths of our souls.

    On a basic level, this process begins with reflecting on the truth of Hashem's existence during davening. At this time, a Yid explains to himself ideas about Hashem until he begins to understand and feel the deep connection to Hashem hidden in his *neshamah*. The Rebbe reveals the depth of our *neshamah* so we can tap into it and internalize that connection through proper reflection during davening and consequently throughout the day.

    See the *maamar Ki Sisa*, 5711 (Toras Menachem, Vol. 2, pp. 257ff), where this aspect of internalizing our faith is explained at length.

HOW TO USE THIS *SEFER*

🙠 Gradated Approach to Davening

R. Nissan Nemanov once remarked: "Just like there are different classes in learning, according to each individual's age and mental capabilities, there should be different 'classes' in davening as well. Each individual should be expected to be on a different level in davening, according to his age and mental capabilities. It would be embarrassing for a twenty-year-old student to be on the same level of learning as a thirteen-year-old. Similarly, it should be embarrassing for someone who is twenty years old to daven in the same way as a thirteen-year-old."

The application from this is obvious. There must be a gradated approach to working on oneself in davening that progresses as a person grows in life.

🙠 Three Age Groups

In general, there are three time frames for working on davening.

1. A child before Bar Mitzvah must learn two basic things:
   a. How to read and pronounce the words properly.
   b. The basic translation of the words of davening.[3]

---

3. See Hayom Yom, 8 Teves:

2. A *bochur* after Bar Mitzvah[4] should work on the following four aspects:

"The Tzemach Tzedek instructed the teachers of his young grandchildren to teach them, in addition to their regular studies, the basic meaning of the order of davening. Once a month, they would come to the Tzemach Tzedek to be tested on this subject." See also the Frierdiker Rebbe's account in *Lekutei Dibburim*, Vol. 3, pp. 989–990 (Hebrew ed.). pp. 271–272 (English ed.):

"Twice, my revered father, the Rebbe [Rashab], learned with me the translation of the words of davening—the weekday davening, the Shabbos and Yom Tov davening, the Hagadah Shel Pesach, and some of the passages of the Rosh Hashanah and Yom Kippur davening. The first time was in my childhood years, and the second time was from my Bar Mitzvah, on the 12th of Tammuz, 5653, and onwards.

"When my father began to teach me the translation of the words of davening for the first time, he said: 'Davening without knowing what you are saying is pointless.' He then proceeded to teach me the basic translation of the words of davening."

4. Obviously, a girl after Bas Mitzva must also continue to advance in davening. It is beyond the scope of this *sefer* to delineate the differences in *chinuch* between boys and girls and how they apply to davening in particular. However, we will suffice with a few short points that are worthy of mentioning here:

   a. The mitzvos of knowing Hashem, recognizing His Oneness, loving and fearing Him, and serving Him with our heart in prayer apply to men and women equally. It thus follows that the study of Chassidus and the proper reflection upon its teachings are also equally necessary for both groups, since only by doing this can one fulfill these mitzvos.

   b. The fact that we learn many fundamental laws of davening from Chana demonstrates that Jewish women excel in the true meaning of davening beyond what men can understand, and therefore it is they who must learn from the women. However, this natural capability will only flourish if it is properly cultivated.

   c. Since the exact laws of how much women are obligated to say and how they must say it are more lenient than they are for men, it is clear that their main focus should be on the *kavanah* and inwardness of davening, more than on the actual recitation of the words.

   d. Women are naturally more inclined to do what Hashem wants and to live more strongly with their simple faith in Hashem. It is therefore clear that they do not need *as much* contemplation on Hashem's greatness to become inspired to truly desire to fulfill His will. However, to whatever extent needed for the specific individual, *some type of reflection is still required*, since this is the only way one can fulfill the mitzvos mentioned above.

a. To concentrate on thinking the meaning of the words of davening while saying them.[5]
b. To study the deeper meaning of the words of the davening and how he can apply it to his life.[6]
c. To reflect for at least a short time on the fact that Hashem is here with him and is constantly watching him, and to realize to Whom he is about to daven.[7]

(See *Lekutei Sichos*, Vol. 26, pp. 267 ff., about the natural tendency of women to fulfill Hashem's will. See ibid., Vol. 30, pp. 145 ff., about their strong faith in Hashem. See also *El N'shei U'Bnos Yisroel*, Chapter One, at length.)

These points are merely general perspectives that require greater elaboration. Accordingly, each woman should ask her *mashpia* how to apply the ideas discussed in this *sefer* to her situation.

5. See Section 2, Chapters 2–4.
6. See Section 2, Chapter 7. See also the continuation of the Frierdiker Rebbe's account quoted above (note 3), describing the study with his father that began after his Bar Mitzvah:

"The second time around, my father taught me the *chassidishe* translation of the words. I am not referring to the printed works of Chabad Chassidus that explain the words of davening (such as *Pirush Hamilos* of the Mitteler Rebbe), rather I am referring to the *chassidishe* explanation of the davening. He explained every verse from *Modeh Ani* and onward according to Chassidus, in a manner that can actually be applied to one's life. For every concept my father would tell me stories, most of which were teachings the Alter Rebbe had received from the Baal Shem Tov and the Maggid of Mezeritch, as well as the explanations of the Alter Rebbe himself and the subsequent Rebbeim."

(The Frierdiker Rebbe continues that after close to two years of study, they only reached the *lesheim yichud* before *Baruch She'amar*. This was obviously a very serious study!)

It is clear from this source that the study of the meaning of the davening this second time around didn't consist of advanced Chassidic teachings, rather of a deeper look at davening and how it can be applied to one's life, based on *chassidishe* stories and teachings.

7. This is a halacha stated clearly in Shulchan Aruch (*Orach Chaim* §98): "Before prayer a person should reflect upon the greatness of Hashem." On a basic level, this applies to anyone over Bar Mitzvah, just like everything else stated in Shulchan Aruch.

See *Reb Shlomo Chaim*, Chapter 4, pp. 292, 298 ff., for advice to *bochurim* of this age group how to train themselves into doing this.

d. To reflect before going to sleep for at least a short time on how he acted that day and how he can do better.[8]

3. Approximately between the ages of sixteen[9] and eighteen,[10] one should begin to advance[11] primarily in two aspects:

   a. To think deeply into the teachings of Chassidus until they make a fundamental change in his way of thinking and feeling (called *hisbonenus*).

   b. To think deeply (not only about how he acted that day, but also) into how he is living his life and if he is truly fulfilling his mission (called a *cheshbon hanefesh* or *cheshbon tzedek*). He should reflect on whether he is truly accomplishing in learning, has good *middos*, trusts in Hashem, is positively influencing his surroundings, and so on.

Making Up for Lacking Steps

All the above is a process that must be built up, each step built on the previous one. If you train yourself to daven on a basic level, you can then proceed to a deeper and more ad-

---

8. This is also a halacha stated in Shulchan Aruch (*Magen Avraham* 239:7. *Kitzur Shulchan Aruch* 71:3).
9. The Alter Rebbe (*Hilchos Talmud Torah* 1:6) quotes from the Gemara that a father is responsible to train his son how to truly fear Hashem starting from the age of sixteen. The reason for this is because before this age a child isn't old enough to truly appreciate what his father is telling him. We see from this that starting from the age of sixteen an adolescent can begin to truly appreciate what it means to fear Hashem.
10. I heard from R. Yitzchok Meir Gurary that starting at around the age of eighteen, the Rebbe would encourage *bochurim* at *yechidus* to daven *ba'arichus* and begin working on themselves *(avodah pnimis)*.
11. I.e., in addition to the four aspects he was working on until this point, he should add significantly in these two areas.

vanced level. However, if you have not yet accomplished what was relevant in your younger years, you will first need to make up what you are lacking before advancing to the level of davening expected at your present age. (This can be compared to someone who is twenty years old and does not yet know how to learn Gemara with Rashi on his own. Such a person must first master this skill before he can proceed to learning Gemara with commentaries.)

For example, if someone did not learn how to pronounce the words of davening properly or their basic translation, he will not be able to reflect upon their deeper meaning. Similarly, if someone didn't work on being able to focus on the meaning of the words and think through an idea of Hashem's greatness for two minutes, he will not be able to daven *ba'arichus*.

However, there is a difference between an adult who needs to backtrack and start from the beginning and a child who is beginning to learn how to daven. An adult in such a situation must work on several aspects simultaneously. He can't wait until he finishes learning the meaning of the words before starting to think about Hashem or making a *cheshbon hanefesh*. Instead, he will need to have three "tracks" of davening, meaning that he will need to work on three aspects simultaneously: (a) thinking about the meaning of the words, (b) thinking Chassidus before davening, and (c) making a *cheshbon hanefesh* before sleeping. He will need to work on a little bit of each of these three aspects every day, until he reaches the level he is truly capable of attaining in davening.[12]

---

12. We find a similar idea regarding Torah study. Ideally, one should learn the entire Tanach from the age of five until ten, then the entire Mishna from ten until fifteen, and then proceed to learn Gemara. However, an adult who has not done so must divide his Torah study into three parts: Tanach, Mishna (or halacha without explanations), and Gemara (or halacha with explanations). The

ஐ For Whom Is This *Sefer* Intended?

This *sefer* is intended for anyone above the age of Bar Mitzvah. The main emphasis for younger adolescents should be on the first two sections, where they will learn about simple sincerity in davening and how to concentrate on the meaning of the words. Although not everything in the third and fourth sections yet apply to them, they can learn from these sections how to start working on thinking about Hashem and how to improve themselves.

(The first section of the *sefer* which discusses simple sincerity in davening isn't a "track" as much as an essential awareness, that every aspect of davening is an expression of the simple, essential connection of a Jew to Hashem, which causes him to want to work on davening. This is something we must always remember and be aware of.[13])

Older adolescents and adults can use all sections of the *sefer* to learn how to work on davening in all three "tracks" mentioned above. Primarily, they will be able to learn how to contemplate on Chassidus in a real way so that it will affect them, and how to look deeply into their lives in a genuine way and perform *teshuvah* with joy.

At any stage you are holding in davening, or if you are holding at the beginning and need to start working on davening, this *sefer* can assist you by helping you divide your davening into these three "tracks," so you can see where you are holding in each "track" and where you can proceed.

---

reason for this is because since a person doesn't know how long he will live, he can't wait until he finishes one section before continuing with the next (see the Alter Rebbe's *Hilchos Talmud Torah* 2:1).

13. See Hayom Yom, 11 Tishrei: "Davening with simple faith connects the essence of the soul to the essence of Hashem."

GENERAL INTRODUCTION

❦ What is Real Davening?

The Frierdike Rebbe once described in a *sichah*[14] what davening is all about:

> Years ago—I don't mean hundreds of years ago, but tens of years ago—there existed the concept of the *avodah* of *tefillah*. [My intention is] not that people would daven at length for a few hours; perhaps only for fifteen to twenty minutes, but it was [actual] davening. First, before davening a person would learn a bit of Chassidus; not a lot, perhaps just a few lines, maybe even only four or five lines, but he would work with them. When he would put on his *tallis gadol* and the tallis was still on his shoulder, he would think over [the few lines he had learnt], and during *tefillah* he would daven. But nowadays . . .
>
> I would now like to speak to the Temimim, the students in the yeshiva.
>
> A person can only be described as "older" if he works on himself and grows. If someone doesn't work on himself, then only his body grows older, but in essence he remains an "old child."
>
> There are students who learn Chassidus and want to understand Chassidus. To them I say: If you want to understand Chassidus, then daven! Davening doesn't mean singing; davening doesn't mean crying. Rather, in daven-

---

14. *Sefer Hasichos* 5705, pp. 113–115.

ing a person should sing a *nigun;* in davening a person should cry.¹⁵

I don't mean to daven for hours; [I mean] just to actually daven.

In general one must guard the times of learning *nigleh* and Chassidus. [Davening] shouldn't contradict the schedule of the yeshiva.

And I don't mean [to daven in a real manner] every day, rather from time to time, especially on Shabbos, which is the opportune time to daven. To daven with *pirush hamilos* is required by all of the *tefillos*—and fortunate is he who davens entirely from the siddur—but here I mean the *avodah* of davening. [It is this type of davening that must happen from time to time.]¹⁶

The question is, so what *is* real davening? It's not just to think the meaning of the words; it's not just to daven for a long time; it's not to sing; and it's not to cry. So what is it?

❧ "Know Before Whom You Stand"

The answer to this question lies in the saying of *Chazal*: "דע לפני מי אתה עומד—Know before Whom you stand." Real davening means to understand what it means to speak to Hashem, to acquire a recognition of Hashem, and to forge a connection with Hashem in one's mind and heart. As the Rebbe writes in a number of letters, the meaning of "Know

---

15. The *sichah* then continues: "Our Sages say that 'the sound [of the words a person says] arouses his intention.' We once explained this saying [in a non-literal manner] as follows: the intention a person has in davening arouses him to the sound of the *nigun* he should sing."
16. The *sichah* then continues to explain that in order to accomplish this, the *avodah* of *Krias Shema Al Hamitah* is necessary, and one must also avoid *chitzoniyus* and *blitos*. A person must really care about davening and not daven merely for others to see, and he must avoid attracting undue attention.

before Who you stand" isn't only to have a basic knowledge that you are standing before the One who can fulfill your requests, but that one must acquire a recognition of Him as well, which is accomplished through studying Chassidus. To quote one such letter (written by the Rebbe in English):[17]

> . . . in order that it [your prayers] be on the proper level, it is necessary to bear in mind "Know before Whom though art standing," which in turn requires preparatory study of the Torah and of the inner aspects of the Torah, which discuss G-d's greatness, and majesty, and wonders, etc. Such study must, of course, be in the proper spirit, namely with a view to translate it into actions and deeds in the daily life.

As is clear from this letter, learning Chassidus before davening enables one to acquire a better understanding of the One before Whom he is about to speak. This idea of acquiring knowledge of Hashem and connecting to Him is what real davening is about. And when one achieves a true recognition of and connection to Hashem, he will also sing and cry: being that his greatest enjoyment lies in knowing and connecting to Hashem, he will sing; and the experience can be so intense that he might cry.

❦ LOVE AND AWE

Now that we know that davening is all about developing a deeper awareness of Hashem, we can look at the effects davening is supposed to have on a person. The Alter Rebbe explains in Tanya[18] that *daas*, knowledge of Hashem, is the result of thinking about Hashem constantly and intensely.

---

17. Dated 10 Sivan 5725.
18. Chapter 3.

This type of thinking produces two feelings: love of Hashem and awe of Him. So since real davening means to acquire *daas*—"Know before Whom you stand," it will cause a person to be aroused with these two feelings.[19]

What does it mean to love Hashem and fear Him? The answer to this can be found in Hayom Yom:[20]

> Just like the mitzvah of tefillin, for example, has a fixed place on the head and arm, and the person who wears them can feel the weight of the head-tefillin and the tightness of the arm-tefillin, so too is with regard to the mitzvos of loving and fearing Hashem. As the Rambam writes (*Hilchos Yesodei Hatorah,* Chapter 2, halacha 1): "It is a mitzvah to love and fear the Exalted and Awesome G-d, as it says, *'You shall love Hashem your G-d'* and *'You shall fear Hashem your G-d.'* " The extent of these mitzvos is that they should be actually felt in one's physical heart.
>
> [Tangible love] can be compared to [what is felt by] one who meets a dear friend. Not only does he feel good as a result and forgets about all the things that are bothering him, but he also becomes rejuvenated with a strong feeling of hope [that things will work out for the good], since he feels good [just by meeting him. Similarly, realizing that you are in the presence of Hashem should energize you and cause you to feel good and full of hope and to forget about what's bothering you.]

---

19. The Alter Rebbe (Tanya, ibid.) compares the knowledge of Hashem to the union between a husband and wife. This is based on the Torah's description of the union between Adam and Chavah with the word "know"—"*And Adam knew his wife Chavah,*" meaning that they bonded to the extent of producing children. Similarly, to "know" Hashem means to connect one's mind to the awareness of Hashem to the extent that tangible feelings will be produced, which will then express themselves in practical application.
20. 20 Menachem Av. The bracketed additions are from the author.

This applies to fear of Hashem as well. A person should feel a great awe and fear [of being in Hashem's presence], as he remembers his misdeeds in thought, speech, and action, and his heart should ache tangibly with pain from the fear of the [spiritual] punishment [for transgressing Hashem's Will[21]], resulting from a fear of Heaven. Sometimes he can experience [a higher level of fear of Hashem—] a feeling of embarrassment [from being in Hashem's Presence], or even a fear of the Exaltedness of Hashem.

In other words, to love and fear Hashem means to realize that Hashem's presence in one's life is a reality that can be felt in a practical sense. And this comes about by really davening, to recognize and feel that Hashem is real and to connect to Him.

There is a famous analogy that brings out this point.[22]

There was once a simple villager who was illiterate. Whenever he would receive a letter, he would ask the local *melamed* to read it to him. One day he received a letter carrying the unfortunate news that his father had passed away. Upon hearing this from the *melamed* (who was reading the letter), the villager fainted on the spot. Later on, people asked the *melamed* why he didn't faint as well. "After all," they surmised, "it was you who was actually reading the letter!", "The letter wasn't about *my* father," the *melamed* replied. "It was about *his* father!"

The lesson we can take from this story is that even if we're dealing with the same information, it won't affect you if you

---

21. I.e., becoming distanced from Hashem.
22. This analogy is mentioned in Toras Menachem (Vol. 42, pp. 164 ff.), as well as in several other places with slight differences.

don't feel that it's relevant to you. Davening means to know and recognize that Hashem is real and relevant in our lives.

❧ Steps in a Process

This is also what lies behind the numerous sections of the daily davening, beginning with *Modeh Ani* and reaching a climax by *Shemonah Esrei*. The various parts of davening are steps of a process, helping us gain awareness of Hashem one step at a time. We begin by saying *Modeh Ani* and the morning *Brachos* to attain a general awareness of Hashem's presence in our lives, and we continue to climb the ladder of knowledge of Hashem until we reach *Shemonah Esrei*, when we achieve the ultimate awareness of "Know before Whom you stand."

The entire davening thus fits within this context, to enable us to "know" Hashem and strengthen and deepen our connection to Him. And this brings about two feelings—love and awe: love, the result of realizing how wonderfully good Hashem is in general and to me in particular, and awe and respect of His greatness.

In truth, even just thinking into the words of davening can help you along this process, even if you don't think through a *maamar* while davening. As long as you prepare yourself and realize what you are trying to accomplish—to achieve an awareness of and develop feelings for Hashem— you can receive all that depth from the words of davening themselves. This is what the Frierdiker Rebbe meant when he said that people used to daven for even just fifteen to twenty minutes, but it was real davening, because they prepared themselves to take it seriously and be affected by it.

Four Components of Real Davening

In order to achieve real davening, it is important to analyze the various components of such a davening and get a picture of the ideas that are involved. For the purpose of this *sefer*, I have divided davening into four essential components; when a person will work on all four areas, he will be able to achieve real davening, with Hashem's help. The four sections of the *sefer* reflect these four components.[23]

1. **Asking and thanking Hashem for one's needs.** Before attaining an advanced understanding of Hashem's greatness, a person must first cultivate a simple, basic awareness of Hashem's presence by simply speaking to Him, asking Him for what he needs and thanking Him for what He has given. The Baal Shem Tov greatly praised this type of simplicity; however, it can be harder to develop in this day and age when people are more complex.

2. **Understanding the meaning of the words of davening.** It is not enough to speak to Hashem in one's own words; one must use the words established by our *Chachomim* in the siddur, as this terminology is the Divine language of the soul. But in order for that to ac-

---

23. These four components are based on the *maamar* "*Rava Chazya LeRav Hamnuna*" 5690 (printed in *Sefer Hamaamorim Kuntreisim*, Vol. 1, p. 217). In this *maamar* the Frierdiker Rebbe explains that davening consists of three aspects: to ask Hashem for what one needs (which is the basic mitzvah of davening), to look in the siddur and think the *pirush hamilos*, and to approach davening with *deveikus* and *teshuvah*. The first two aspects correspond to the first two components described below, while the third aspect can be divided in two—*deveikus*, connecting to Hashem while davening *Shacharis* (especially through *hisbonenus*), and *teshuvah*, accomplished mainly through making a *cheshbon hanefesh* by Krias Shema Al Hamitahh. These two ideas correspond to the third and fourth components.

tually mean something to a person, he must understand and think into the meaning of the words.

3. **Learning and contemplating Chassidus.** In order to know before Whom one is standing, one must learn about and develop an awareness of Him. Learning doesn't just mean to read words in a book; it means to understand and connect to those ideas until they become part of you.

4. **Making a *cheshbon hanefesh*.** Since the main goal of davening is to be inspired to fulfill Hashem's will through Torah and mitzvos, it thus follows that an important part of davening is to be constantly aware of one's standing in *avodas Hashem*. For this to happen, one must frequently make a *cheshbon hanefesh*.

Section 1:
BASIC DAVENING

Chapter 1.
REQUESTING AND THANKING HASHEM FOR OUR NEEDS

Every Jew possesses an inherent belief that Hashem is the Creator and Master of the world. This belief dictates that a person should ask Hashem for whatever he needs whenever he needs it, since He alone is the One who can provide him with his needs. Similarly, one must thank Hashem for what He has given him, since everything a person has comes from Hashem Himself (although He utilizes various channels to direct His blessings to us).

It is a *mitzvah min hatorah*[24] to ask Hashem for whatever you might need, and this is something you must constantly do. For this reason, a person asks Hashem for anything he might need three times a day in *Shemonah Esrei*. Halacha also allows one to add additional requests when saying the middle blessings of *Shemonah Esrei* (i.e., from *Chonen Hada'as* until *Shema Koleinu*), provided the content of the request is similar to the content of that particular blessing (for example, in the blessing of *Refa'ainu* one can ask Hashem to cure a specific person).[25] In the blessing of *Shema Kolainu* and after *Shemonah*

---

24. According to the Rambam this is a *mitzvah* that must be performed daily, while the Ramban is of the opinion that one must do so only when one feels a particular need. See the beginning of Shoresh Mitzvas Hatefillah (*Derech Mitzvosecha*, p. 229) where the different opinions are brought.

25. שו"ע או"ח סי' קי"ט ס"א.

Esrei (before the second *Yihiyu Leratzon*) one may add any request.[26]

You should accustom yourself to ask Hashem at least three times a day to help you with whatever is bothering you.[27] This means to simply ask Hashem for what you need or really desire, whether physical requests[28] (for example, to provide financial means and the like) or spiritual ones (for example, to assist in understanding Torah, doing proper *teshuvah*, developing *ahavas yisroel*, and so on). Even if you have already davened that day, you should ask Hashem for assistance if you need something in particular, and you should rely on Him to help you.[29]

The same applies to thanking Hashem for what He has given you. In addition to saying *Modim* during *Shemonah Esrei*,[30] you should thank Hashem in your own words throughout the day, and particularly when you see how He has given you what you need.

---

26. In a letter dated 11 *Shevat* 5746 (printed in *Likutei Sichos* Vol. 39 p. 281), the Rebbe says that "requests for healing for specific individuals should be added in *Shema Kolainu*. You should consult the Rav of your city for more details."
    The Rebbe was of the opinion that as a rule, one should limit inserting additional requests to *Shema Kolainu*, as opposed to the other *brachos* (heard from R. Yitzchak Meir Gurary).
27. A suggested time to do this is when saying *Shema Koleinu* (during the week) or before the second *Yihiyu Leratzon* (both during the week and on Shabbos or Yom Tov) where Halacha allows one to add personal requests.
28. We see a similar idea from the statement of the *Zohar* that R' Yaisa would ask Hashem to provide him with food, even though the food was already prepared and ready to eat. See *Lekutei Sichos* (Vol. 26, p. 95) for an explanation of this idea.
29. This idea is based on the opinion of the Ramban (see fn. 24) that the mitzvah of *tefillah min hatorah* is to request for help whenever there's something in particular that's bothering you.
30. You should realize that Hashem's kindness is with you every moment, and you should thank Him for helping you continuously. This theme is expressed in the words of *Modim:* נודה לך ונספר תהלתך על חיינו המסורים בידך ועל נשמותינו הפקודות לך, ועל נסיך שבכל יום עמנו ועל נפלאותיך וטובותיך שבכל עת, ערב ובקר וצהרים.

A central idea in asking Hashem for assistance and thanking Him is that a person can talk to Him as he would talk to another individual *kevayochol*. This is an essential concept in *avodas Hashem*—to recognize that Hashem is real, at least as real as a person *kevayochol*.[31] A person may fulfill mitzvos simply because he was instructed to do so by his parents and teachers, and not necessarily because of a conscious recognition of the presence of Hashem. You must therefore strive as much as possible to view Hashem as being real, and one of the basic ways of accomplishing this is by constantly talking to Hashem. This is also the reason why *Chazal* instituted the many prayers and blessings we say every day and directed us to recite one hundred *brachos* daily, so that our awareness of Hashem's presence will increase.[32]

This idea—that we must relate to Hashem with simplicity and pray to Him as would a child[33]—is a fundamental concept in Yiddishkeit in general and in Chassidus in particular. The Baal Shem Tov would urge people to say words of praise to Hashem in their own language and constantly say "with Hashem's help," "*Boruch Hashem*," and similar phrases. He revealed that these simple words are more powerful and effective Above than the mystical *kavanos* of the *mekubalim*.[34]

There is a difference between *Chagas Chassidus* and *Chabad Chassidus* in the correct approach to this idea. *Chagas Chassidus* focuses on the concept of speaking to Hashem as a fundamental part of *avodas Hashem*, while *Chabad Chassidus*, which emphasizes the use of one's mind to understand

---

31. See Shabbos (28b) where R' Yochanan Ben Zakai tells his students: "You should fear Hashem as much as you would a person. Just as one refrains from sin when a person is watching, so should one be constantly aware of Hashem's presence and refrain from sin."
32. שו"ע אדה"ז סי' מו ס"א.
33. שו"ת ריב"ש סי' קנ"ז.
34. ספר השיחות תש"ג ע' 163 ואילך.

Hashem, doesn't put as much of an emphasis on focusing on this concept. However, the difference is only regarding *how much* emphasis is placed,[35] but the actual idea is as important according to *Chabad Chassidus* as well. Additionally, *Chabad Chassidus* demands that we should try to understand the value of talking to Hashem with simplicity,[36] and explains that by realizing that our physical necessities come from Hashem and thanking Him for them, we can achieve the ultimate fulfillment of *dirah betachtonim*.[37]

Thus, the most basic idea of davening is to simply talk to Hashem, to ask Him for what we need and thank and praise Him for what He does for us.

---

35. A practical difference between *Chagas Chassidus* and *Chabad Chassidus* in this regard is that according to *Chabad Chassidus*, when you speak to Hashem you don't necessarily need to speak loudly or for a specific amount of time, and in general there is more of a focus on avoiding *chitzoniyus* and *blitos*.

36. ראה ד"ה באתי לגני תשכ"ט ס"ח בעניין ואתה קדוש יושב תהלות ישראל.

37. ראה לקו"ש ח"ז ס"ע 136 ואילך.

Chapter 2.
THINKING ABOUT HASHEM THROUGHOUT THE DAY

There is an entire *siman* in Shulchan Aruch dedicated (as expressed in its title) to explaining "that all of one's intentions should be *lesheim shamayim*."[38] The Shulchan Aruch explains that one should not engage in physical activities—such as eating, drinking, sleeping, exercising, conducting business, and so on—for one's personal pleasure; rather, one should have in mind that he is doing these activities to be able to serve Hashem. For example, when eating one should have in mind that he is eating to have the strength to serve Hashem. Similarly, before going to sleep he should have in mind that he is resting in order to regain strength to serve Hashem. When doing laundry he should think that he is cleaning his clothing to be able to serve Hashem. The idea is that you should think about Hashem as many times throughout the day as possible, which will lead you to a state of constant focus on Hashem. (As mentioned in Chapter 1, this is why *Chazal* instituted that we should recite one hundred *brachos* throughout the day.)

Just as you should train yourself to think the *pirush hamilos* of davening (as explained in Section 2), so should you train yourself to focus on Hashem constantly and have Him in mind before every activity you perform. Asking and thanking Hashem for your needs throughout the day (as explained

---

38. שו"ע או"ח סי' רלא.

in Chapter 1) is also part of being constantly aware that whatever you has comes from Hashem. The Baal Shem Tov explains that on a certain level, this is the idea of constant *deveikus*, to always be focused on Hashem.[39]

---

39. עיין צוואת הריב"ש סי' פא.

Section 2:
PIRUSH HAMILOS

Chapter 1.
CONCENTRATING ON THE *PIRUSH HAMILOS* OF THE SET *TEFILOS*

Although it is important to speak to Hashem in one's own words (as explained in the previous section), it is just as essential, if not more, to understand the *pirush hamilos* of the *tefilos* instituted by *Chazal*.

The reason for this is because the average person isn't (fully) in touch with the feelings of his *nefesh ha'elokis* and consequently we lack the means to express ourselves properly to Hashem on our own. Because of this deficiency, *Chazal* established the language of the *tefilos*, using *ruach hakodesh* and integrating *pesukim* from Tanach, thus enabling every person to properly praise and thank Hashem and ask Him for what he needs. These *tefilos* contain whatever sentiment one might possibly want to express to Hashem, and they express them in a much more powerful way than one can express them on his own. Therefore, despite the importance of talking to Hashem in one's own words, it is critical to understand the *pirush hamilos* of these *tefilos* and to communicate to Hashem through them.

It is important to underscore this point, namely, that the goal is to communicate with Hashem particularly through the words of davening and Tehillim, as these words contain a unique *kedushah* and reveal a person's *neshamah*. Speaking to Hashem in one's own words is merely (1) a temporary method of communication that should be used until a person starts taking davening more seriously; and (2) a way to enhance the regular davening and help one realize that he is actually speaking to Hashem. Additionally, a simple person who is unable to understand the *pirush hamilos* of davening can speak to Hashem in his own words. But someone who has the ability to understand and feel what he is saying should try his utmost to do so. We can pour out our hearts and souls when davening and saying Tehillim if we would only connect to it and take it personally.

There are times when you can and should express yourself on your own, such as (1) when adding a specific request in *Shemonah Esrei*, and (2) when asking and thanking Hashem throughout the day. But the main method of communicating to Hashem is by reciting the holy words of davening and Tehillim.

Three Levels of Importance in *Kavanah*

The various parts of davening can be divided into three levels, based on how significant a role *kavanah* plays when saying them. The first level includes the parts of davening one is not *yotzei* without *kavanah*, and they must be repeated if they were recited without concentration. The second level includes the parts of davening where there is a Halachic doubt if one has fulfilled his obligation without *kavanah*, and one should therefore be especially careful to have *kavanah* when reciting them. The third level consists of the parts of davening where it is strongly recommended to have *kavanah*, but *bedi'eved*, one has fulfilled his obligation even if he didn't have *kavanah*.

It goes without saying that it is important to have *kavanah* during the entire davening (even when saying those parts that aren't included in one of these three categories). But it's important to have a *seder* in *avodas Hashem*, meaning that you have to know where to start and where to continue. For this reason, you need to have priorities in davening: first you should accomplish what is most important and then you can continue to the next step. Being aware of these three levels can assist in doing this, so you can first work on concentrating on the parts of davening that belong to the first level and then continue with the second and third levels. Chassidus explains that davening is like a ladder; this process is also part of the ladder of davening.

First level. It is of primary importance to concentrate on the *pirush hamilos* of the parts of davening where lack of *kavanah* is *me'akev bedi'eved*. Halacha lists three things as belonging to this category: (1) the first *brachah* of *Shemonah Esrei*; (2) the first two verses of *Krias Shema* (i.e., from *"shema"* until *"va'ed"*); and (3) the *possuk* פותח את ידיך ומשביע לכל חי רצון (in *Pesukei Dezimra*). If one didn't have *kavanah* by any of these three sections, he must go back and repeat them.[40] It is there-

---

40. See Shulchan Aruch (*Orach Chaim* 51:7; 63:4 and commentaries), regarding *Shema* and *posei'ach es yadecha*.

Regarding *Shemonah Esrei*, the Mechaber rules that one should go back and repeat the first *brachah* if he didn't have *kavanah*, while the Rama says that one should not repeat it, because it is likely that he won't have *kavanah* the second time as well (ibid. 101:1). However, one should not infer from this that it is not as important to have *kavanah* during the first *brachah* of *Shemonah Esrei*. Just the opposite, this halacha demonstrates the importance of having *kavanah*, to the extent that he hasn't fulfilled his obligation. But he cannot fix the problem by repeating *Shemonah Esrei*, since he might lack *kavanah* once again and will have said *Shemonah Esrei* twice in vain (as opposed to *Shema* and *posei'ach es yadecha*, where there is no issue of *brachah levatalah*). This demonstrates the importance of having *kavanah* the first time.

(Additionally, even according to the Rama one can sometimes be required to repeat *Shemonah Esrei* due to lack of *kavanah*. The commentaries [*Mishnah Berurah* and *Shaar Hatziyun*, Orach Chaim 96:1] write that someone who normally has *kavanah* but was distracted by something beyond his control [like a ringing cell phone] should repeat *Shemonah Esrei*, since his lack of concentration wasn't his fault and he will have *kavanah* when he repeats it.)

fore of utmost importance to have *kavanah* when saying each word of these three sections. (This can be done either while saying the words, before saying each word or two, or after reciting each word or two, as explained in Chapter 3.)

Second level. This level includes the numerous *brachos* recited during davening and over the course of the day.

The Alter Rebbe cites a Halachic argument regarding how much *kavanah* is needed when saying a *brachah*.[41] Some say that one does not fulfill his obligation at all unless he has a minimal amount of *kavanah*, while others say that one has fulfilled his obligation without *kavanah*. The Alter Rebbe concludes that this is a matter of Halachic doubt, and therefore one must be extremely careful to have *kavanah* by all *brachos*. This is especially true regarding *Birchas Hamazon*, as it is possible that one has not fulfilled an obligation *min hatorah*. (Even by any other *brachah* which is *midrabanan*, saying a *brachah* without *kavanah* may be a *brachah levatalah* G-d forbid.)

The Alter Rebbe lists four parts of each *brachah* that require *kavanah* to fulfill one's obligation:

1. The words (אתה) ברוך.[42]
2. Hashem's Name; i.e., the words ה' אלקינו (or just 'ה if אלקינו is not said, such as at the conclusion of a long *brachah*).
3. Hashem's Kingship; i.e., the words מלך העולם.
4. The content of the *brachah*; for example, the words בורא פרי האדמה.

In a long *brachah*, namely, one that both starts and concludes with *boruch* (such as *Al Hamichyah*), having *kavanah* is mandatory only at the beginning and end of the *brachah*. In

---

41. שו"ע או"ח סי' קפה ס"ב.
42. It is unclear if the word אתה requires *kavanah* as well.

other words, you must concentrate on the above four parts at the beginning of the *brachah* and on three parts at the end (where מלך העולם is not mentioned), while concentrating on the text in the middle isn't *me'akev*. The same applies for any other long *brachah*, such as *Asher Yatzar, Kiddush Levanah,* and *Hama'avir Sheinah Mei'einay.*

Thus, when *bentching,* it would be mandatory to have *kavanah* for the following parts: (1) the beginning and end of the first *brachah;* (2) the end of the second and third *brachos* (but not the beginning, because these *brachos* are said as a continuation of the preceding *brachah*[43] and don't start with *boruch*); and (3) the beginning of the fourth *brachah* (which doesn't conclude with *boruch*).[44]

Regarding *Pesukei Dezimra* and *Birchos Krias Shema,* it would be mandatory to have *kavanah* for the following: (1) the beginning and end of *Boruch She'amar;* (2) the end of *Yishtabach;*[45] (3) the beginning and end of *Yotzer Ohr;* and (4) the end

---

43. Known as a *brachah hasmuchah lachavertah.*
44. It would seem that the content of the fourth *brachah* is mainly expressed in the words המלך הטוב והמטיב לכל (and not as much in the words 'הא-ל אבינו מלכנו וכו), and it would be these words one would be required to concentrate on, but further investigation is required.

    (To elaborate:

    Several factors indicate that the words המלך הטוב והמטיב לכל express the main content of the *brachah.*
    1. The *brachah* is known as *hatov vehameitiv.*
    2. These words must be said in all forms of the *brachah.* [For example, in the house of a mourner where the text of the fourth *brachah* is changed, these words remain—see Shulchan Aruch, Orach Chaim, 189:2.]
    3. In *Al Hamichyah,* the shortened version of the fourth *brachah* of *Birchas Hamazon* is כי אתה ה' טוב ומטיב לכל.

    Despite these indications, further investigation is still required, as I have yet to find a definite source that these words are the most important in the context of having *kavanah.*)
45. It would seem that the content of *Yishtabach* is mainly expressed in the words א-ל מלך גדול ומהולל בתשבחות, and it would be these words one would be required to concentrate on, but further investigation is required.

of *Ahavas Olam* and *Emes Veyatziv* (i.e., ברוך וכו' גאל ישראל). The same would apply to *Birchos Krias Shema* by Maariv.

In short *brachos* (that only begin with *boruch*), such as the morning *brachos*, you must have *kavanah* by each one, and lacking *kavanah* might prevent you from being *yotzei*. Similarly, having *kavanah* is mandatory when saying a *brachah* before eating, drinking, and performing a mitzvah. It is therefore very important to have *kavanah* when saying these *brachos*. (Additionally, as explained in Section 1, the reason *Chazal* instituted that we should recite numerous *brachos* throughout the day was to help us be aware of Hashem constantly, and this objective can be attained primarily when we have *kavanah* when saying them.)

Third level. It is important to have *kavanah* by the end of each of the *brachos* of *Shemonah Esrei*. Even though one has fulfilled his obligation even if he has said these *brachos* without *kavanah* (with the exception of the first *brachah* as explained above),[46] it is nonetheless very important to have *kavanah* when saying them.[47]

(To elaborate:

The Shulchan Aruch [Orach Chaim 54:2] cautions that one shouldn't answer *amen* after א-ל מלך גדול ומהולל בתשבחות but rather after חי העולמים since these words constitute the real conclusion of the *brachah*. This implies that the words א-ל מלך גדול ומהולל בתשבחות express the main idea of the *brachah*, and that is why one would think to answer *amen* at that point [but one shouldn't do so since the *brachah* isn't actually over].

Furthermore, the Mishnah Berurah [ibid.] deliberates whether one may interrupt after saying א-ל מלך גדול ומהולל בתשבחות to answer *amen yehai shemai rabba* or *kedushah*, since the main idea has already been expressed.

However, further investigation is still required, as I have yet to find a definite source that these words are the most important in the context of having *kavanah*.)

46. שו"ע אדה"ז סי' קפה ס"ב.
47. שו"ע אדה"ז סי' קא ס"א.

Additionally, the Gemara strongly praises someone who has *kavanah* when saying *yehei shmei rabba*, saying that this causes such happiness by Hashem that He revokes any evil decree against that person.[48] Chassidus explains that saying *yehei shmei rabba* with *kavanah* reveals Hashem's Great Name within this world, referring to the ultimate truth of Hashem that will be revealed when *Moshiach* comes.[49]

The Frierdiker Rebbe relates that when the great *chossid* R. Dovid Tzvi Chein was a boy, his father brought him to the Tzemach Tzedek. The Tzemach Tzedek told him: "Stop being a child. When you make a *brachah*, you must know to Whom you are speaking." From then on, whenever R. Dovid Tzvi recited a *brachah*, he would place his hand on his forehead and think for a moment, and only then would he say the *brachah*, slowly and with *kavanah*.[50]

---

48. שו"ע או"ח סי' נו ס"א.
49. תו"א מג, ג ובכ"מ.
50. סה"ש תש"ג ע' 143 (משיחת ח"י אלול תש"ג).

Chapter 2.
HOW TO DEVELOP *KAVANAH*

Developing *kavanah* in davening is a lifelong *avodah*. Every day a new battle must be fought to daven properly, so that instead of being done by rote it should be filled with meaning. However, as is the case with everything in life, the key to success is to have a *seder*, a planned-out approach how to accomplish this goal. With Hashem's help, the next few chapters will explain some basic ideas how this can be done.

These techniques can be divided into those that deal with the davening itself *(cheftza)*, i.e., to study *tefillah* and divide the davening into sections, and those that focus on the person *(gavra)*, i.e., how to conduct yourself to enable proper concentration. The present chapter will focus mainly on the first category, while the second category will be discussed primarily in Chapter 4.

❦ STUDYING *TEFILLAH*

One who has not yet studied the meaning of the words of davening must begin by taking the time to go through the davening with an English siddur, one section at a time. This is true regardless of your current age. A suggested way to do this, to avoid making it seem tedious and dull, is by focusing on one paragraph of davening every day. You can look at the English translation before saying each word or phrase in that paragraph and think the meaning of what you are about to say. This will enable you to think through the meaning of that paragraph, and the next day you can focus on the next paragraph. (Obviously, it's recommended to start from the beginning of davening and continue in order.) This process can be repeated until you are familiar with the meaning of the words of davening.[51]

This method can also be used to build up an understanding of Tehillim. You can focus on a chapter of Tehillim every day and think through the meaning of the words as described above, and the next day you can continue with the next chapter, until you will master the meaning of the entire Tehillim.[52]

Dividing the Davening

Once you have mastered the meaning of at least most of the words of davening, you are ready to work on the next step—to actually think the meaning of the words you are saying while saying them. Understanding the meaning of the words doesn't necessarily mean you will actually think their meaning while saying them. This is because when a person gets into the habit of saying the same words every day, it becomes second nature for him and he tends to say them without concentrating.[53] Special effort must therefore be put into thinking the meaning of the words while saying them.

---

51. See Chapter 4 where various techniques will be discussed to assist in concentrating on the meaning of the words.
52. I recommend the Artscroll Interlinear Tehillim which has a user-friendly format that makes it much easier to learn the meaning of every word.
53. *Tanya* (*Igeres Hakodesh* §19 p. 257) explains that as a rule, a person can only say something he has previously thought about, because speech is an expression of thought. But nevertheless, if a person is in the habit of saying certain words, he can say them without thinking. The reason for this is because since his thoughts entered these words many times, the words continue to receive their energy from the "imprint" and outer aspect of these thoughts, even if he is not actually concentrating on the words at this time.

However, it's not easy to have *kavanah* for the entire davening every day. You must therefore work out a plan to figure out how to have as much *kavanah* as possible during the time you have available for davening. Three general ideas play a role in forming such a plan: (1) making priorities, (2) focusing on a different part of davening every day, and (3) building up your ability to concentrate.

Making priorities. As explained in Chapter 1, there are certain parts of davening where it is especially important to have *kavanah*, and these parts of davening can be divided into three levels, based on how significant a role *kavanah* plays when saying them. You should therefore begin working on having *kavanah* at the first level, by putting effort into thinking the meaning of the words of the first *brachah* of *Shemonah Esrei*, the first two verses of *Krias Shema*, and the *possuk* of *posei'ach es yadecha*.

You should grow accustomed to the idea that when it comes to these parts of davening, come what may, you will concentrate on the meaning of every word, even if, for whatever reason, you are unable to do so for the rest of davening. After you get used to having *kavanah* for the first level, you should continue with the second and third levels.

Concentrating on a Different Section Every Day. Making priorities as discussed above can help you develop *kavanah* for those parts of davening where you should have *kavanah* every day. Additionally, you should create a cycle in which you will go through the entire davening with *kavanah* by having *kavanah* for one section of davening each day.

It says in *Tanya* that even if one has thought the meaning of each part of davening only once throughout the entire year, it is enough to elevate all the prayers of the year.[54] This demonstrates that creating a cycle is effective even if it consists of having *kavanah* for only a small part of davening each day, to the extent that it takes a complete year to go through the entire davening.

In order for this system to work for both the weekday and Shabbos davening, you should create a separate cycle for each one and keep track of both of them.

Building Up the Ability To Concentrate. Obviously, the ideal goal is to have *kavanah* for the entire davening. But the only way to reach this goal is by working on building up the ability to concentrate for an extended period of time. Doing this takes much time and effort at each stage of growth. It's like a person who works on strengthening his physical muscles; he has to spend time working on each intensity level so that his muscles will grow slowly but surely. Similarly, you must spend time at each stage of *kavanah* development so that your ability to concentrate will continue to grow.

We will present here two alternative approaches how to develop the ability to concentrate:

1. **Increasing the amount of time.** One way to build up concentration is by starting with a short amount of time when you will focus on concentrating, and then expanding on it. For example, you can start by taking five minutes every day when you will think the meaning of every word, regardless of how many, or few, words you end up saying during that time frame. (This isn't that hard to do, because you can tell yourself, "What? I can't control my thoughts for even just five minutes?!")

---

54. קו"א דף קנד, ב.

If you do this every day for a month or more, you can continue with ten minutes of concentration. After working on this for many months (or perhaps a few years if needed), you will grow so accustomed to thinking the meaning of the words that you will be able to think the meaning of all the words of davening in an hour or so.[55]

2. **Increasing the parts of davening.** Another way to build up concentration is to start with taking one part of davening (in addition to the three levels listed above) and think the meaning of every word of that part. Once you get used to concentrating on that part, you can add another part of davening.

For example, you can start from the beginning of *Shemonah Esrei*, and after getting used to thinking the meaning of the first *brachah* (which takes priority over the rest), you can add the next two *brachos* (from *atah gibor* through *hakail hakadosh*) and make sure to think the meaning of these *brachos* as well. When it gets easier to think the meaning of these *brachos*, you can add the next three *brachos*. After many months, you will get used to thinking the meaning of the entire *Shemonah Esrei*, and you can then continue with *Shema* and other parts of davening. After working on this for a few years, you will get used to thinking the meaning of the entire davening.

The common factor between these two approaches is that you must be consistent and have patience to put in the daily struggle to work on developing *kavanah*, and with Hashem's help, you will succeed and grow in davening. Just like every-

---

55. The Rebbe once said that *Shacharis* shouldn't take less than an hour from beginning to end.

thing else in life, you get what you give, and the affect davening will have on you depends on how much effort you put into it.

Chapter 3.
SYNCHRONIZING THE *KAVANAH* WITH THE WORDS

The ultimate goal in davening is to think the meaning of the words while saying them.[56] However, since this may be difficult to actualize, we will divide synchronizing the *kavanah* with the words into two stages:

1. To think the meaning of the words slightly apart from saying them.
2. To think the meaning of the words while actually saying them.

The first stage, where you think the meaning of a few words slightly apart from saying them, is a recommended method when learning the meaning of the words (see Chapter 2, "Studying *Tefillah*"). By doing this, you will get used to thinking the meaning of the words. This is what you should do the first few times you go through the siddur and Tehillim.

We will present here two alternative techniques how to get used to thinking the meaning of the words slightly apart from saying them, so that you will eventually be able to think their meaning while actually saying them:

1. One technique is to think over the meaning of a few words *before* saying them, and then to think it over

---

56. שו"ע אדה"ז או"ח סי' ה: "צריך לכוין הברכות פירוש המילות שמוציא מפיו, וכשיזכיר השם יכוין וכו' ", היינו בעת האמירה, והוא לשון הטור ומחבר (עם שינויים קלים).

again while actually saying them. This may appear difficult, but it isn't as difficult as articulating the meaning of the words in your mind while actually saying them (if you aren't used to doing so).[57]

2. Alternatively, you can first say a few words and *then* think over their meaning.[58] This is not as difficult as thinking beforehand, because here you are thinking the meaning of the words just once (immediately after, instead of both before and while saying them), but it isn't as ideal as thinking beforehand.[59]

(I have personally found this technique to work well for myself, but I have heard from many *mashpi'im* that it's better to think the meaning of the words before saying them.

This can be demonstrated from the following story: When the Frierdiker Rebbe was a young boy, he once asked his grandmother Rebbetzin Rivka why it takes his father such a long time to daven. She an-

---

57. באשל אברהם ובאלי' רבה (או"ח סי' ה) העירו מהבחיי (ויקרא כד, י) שכתב שקודם שיזכיר השם יכוין בו.
וז"ל הבחיי שם: "צריך המברך כשהוא מברך את ה' שיתבונן תחלה בלבו בפירוש אותיות ה', ובמה הן מורות ולכוין בהם במחשבתו, ואח"כ יברך את ה' ויזכירנו בפיו, ועם זה יקבל שכרו משלם ויחיה חיי עד, זכר לדבר מה שכתוב: ארוממך אלקי המלך ואברכה שמך לעולם ועד, יאמר: ארוממך תחלה במחשבתי ובכוונת הלב ואח"כ ואברכה, כענין שאמרו: לעולם יכנס אדם שיעור שני פתחים ואח"כ יתפלל", עכ"ל.

58. עיין שו"ע אדה"ז סי' סא ס"ז, שמביא מתרומת הדשן ומגן אברהם שהפירוש ב"מאריכין באחד" הוא שחושב הענין אחר אמירת התיבה. ועיין רמב"ם הל' נדרים פי"ג הי"ט שיש תוך כדי דיבור לכוונה כמו לדיבור.
ולהעיר מכתר שם טוב [הוצאה החדשה ע' כה] (אות לט): "[ופעם א' שאל השואל למורי זלה"ה אם אמר כמה תיבות בק"ש ובתפלה בלא כוונה אם רשאי לחזור פעם שנית ולאומרם בכוונה, ואמר בזה הלשון: הלא ידוע ומפורסם שאין לך שום דבר שלא יהא בו מציאות השם, אפילו מחשבה חיצונית שם יש ג"כ ניצוצות קדושות כנודע, וא"כ] אם אמר כמה תיבות (בק"ש ו)בתפלה בלא כוונה, לא יאמרם פעם שנית, רק יהרהר במחשבה ובכוונה התיבות שאמר בלא כוונה. כל זה שמעתי [בשם] מורי (הבעש"ט) זלה"ה [ודפח"ח]".

59. See Chapter 4, "Some More Practical Tips" (especially paragraphs 5 and 6), for additional ideas to assist in thinking the meaning of the words.

swered: "Your father is a great chossid and tzaddik, and he thinks the meaning of each word of davening before saying it."[60])

The second stage is when you are already used to thinking the meaning of the words, so you can suffice with concentrating on the meaning while saying them. Since this can be difficult, you should first become familiar with the meaning of the words (by having one or more cycles to go through the davening and learn the meaning of each piece, as explained in Chapter 2). After you are familiar with the meaning of all the words, you should then continue with another cycle (or cycles) in which you will focus on thinking the meaning of the words slightly apart from saying them. When you feel ready for the next step, you should choose a piece of davening every day where you will think the meaning of each word while actually saying it, and slowly expand to additional sections.

If you feel you can begin right away with thinking the meaning of the words while saying them, that's great, and there's definitely nothing wrong with that. But some people might find it hard to start off immediately in this manner and may find it easier to progress in stages as described above.[61]

---

60. *Lekutei Diburim*, Vol. 4, p. 1347.
61. I have not seen this method written explicitly in any *sefer*, but it worked well for me personally, and I hope it will be effective for others as well.

Chapter 4.
PREPARING FOR DAVENING AND STAYING FOCUSED

The only way to have *kavanah* while davening is if you maintain a conduct that is conducive to doing so. We will go through some basic habits (taken mostly from Halacha) that can help a person develop the right frame of mind for davening.

❧ Removing Distractions

1. One shouldn't converse with others excessively before davening. According to one opinion, one shouldn't even greet someone with a "good morning" in the regular fashion, to remind him to avoid entering conversations before davening.[62] This is especially true right before davening, when you should be exclusively involved with learning and thinking Chassidus and the like. (Obviously, even if you want to discuss an idea in Chassidus with someone else, which is fine to do before davening, you shouldn't do so in the place where the minyan is davening, as that will disturb those who are davening.)

---

62. שו"ע או"ח סי' פט ס"ב.

2. One shouldn't hold an object that might distract him.[63] It goes without saying that you should turn off (at least the volume of) your cell phone before davening.
3. The Gemara states that when entering shul, one should first enter the size of two doorways and then begin davening. The Shulchan Aruch cites three explanations of this passage:

   a. One should stand the size of two doorways (i.e., eight *tefachim*) away from the door before davening, to avoid giving the impression that he wants to leave shul immediately after davening. This halacha can be extended to include any action that gives the impression that he wants to leave shul the moment davening is over.

   b. A person shouldn't sit within the size of two doorways (eight *tefachim*) from the door so that he won't be tempted to look outside. This implies that one shouldn't sit in a place where he can easily become distracted.

   c. One should wait the amount of time it takes to walk through two sets of doors before davening. This implies that one shouldn't start to daven the moment he enters the shul, rather he should first stop, wait, and focus for a moment.

   The Shulchan Aruch concludes that one should pay heed to all three explanations and their implications.[64]

   (According to Chassidus, entering the first doorway means to remove worldly thoughts from your

---

63. שו"ע או"ח סי' צו ס"א.
64. או"ח סי' צ ס"כ.

mind, i.e., to clear your mind of all distracting thoughts. Entering the second doorway means to think about and focus on the fact that you are about to speak to Hashem Himself.[65])

4. When learning before davening, one should conclude with something inspiring that will help him daven, and not with something complicated that will occupy his mind and disturb his davening.[66]

Proper Body Position

1. One should sit or stand in one place while davening and not walk around. Some people claim that they have an easier time concentrating when they move around; however, the opposite is true—it makes it harder to concentrate.[67]

2. One should lower his head slightly[68] and look into the siddur[69] while davening.

3. One shouldn't put his hands on his hips during davening, rather they should lie on the table, hold the siddur, be folded over, or the like.[70] One shouldn't sit with his legs crossed when davening.[71] Additionally, one shouldn't lean on his back, lean to the sides, or stretch out his legs.[72]

---

65. קונטרס התפלה פי"א.
66. שו"ע או"ח סי' צג ס"ג.
67. קונטרס התפלה פי"א.
68. שו"ע או"ח סי' צה ס"ב.
69. מג"א סי' צג סק"א.
70. שו"ע או"ח סי' צה ס"ג.
71. קונטרס סדר הנהגה לתלמידים. וכ"כ בבאה"ט או"ח סי' צה סק"ג.
72. באר היטב שם.

Proper Thoughts Before Beginning to Daven

There are two *simanim* in Shulchan Aruch (95 and 98) which discuss how one should focus his thoughts properly before beginning to daven. What follows is a synopsis of these two *simanim*:

1. **Siman 95.** One should turn his eyes downward (toward the siddur) and face Yerushalayim, but in his heart he should focus upward and think that he is speaking directly to Hashem Himself. One should consider as if he is actually standing in the *Beis Hamikdash* and davening to Hashem.

2. **Siman 98.** While davening, one should concentrate on the meaning of the words he is saying. Before beginning to daven, one should view himself as if he is standing before the *shechinah* and remove from his mind all thoughts that trouble him until he can concentrate.

    He should tell himself: If I would be speaking before a king of flesh and blood, I would be very careful with every word I say; how much more so should I be careful when speaking to Hashem! The difference is that before Hashem our thoughts are like words because He hears our thoughts; consequently, we must be as careful with our thoughts before Him as we would be with our words before a human king.

    If a foreign thought comes and disturbs him during davening, he should pause and wait for it to pass before continuing to daven.

    The Rama adds that before davening one should reflect on great Hashem is and how lowly a human being is when compared to Him, until he divests himself from thinking about physical pleasures and instead focuses on connecting to Hashem.

In *Kuntres HaTefillah*,[73] the Rebbe Rashab adds more explanation on how to remove distracting thoughts. If someone claims that he can't remove distracting thoughts from his mind while davening, he should contemplate on the following: When it comes to falling asleep, a person succeeds in removing all disturbing thoughts, since he knows that he needs to sleep. This is because a person can remove distracting thoughts for something that is important. (Some give an example from someone who is learning how to drive a car: when he must focus on the road, he can push away all other thoughts, since his life depends on it.) When he will realize that davening is just as important and is something his *neshamah* needs, he will certainly be able to remove all distracting thoughts.

Upon thinking about this idea a few times, a person will realize that it's within his ability to remove all other thoughts and focus only on davening.

In several letters the Rebbe recommends thinking over the first page of Tanya Chapter 41 before beginning to daven.[74] This can serve as a way of fulfilling the abovementioned directive of the Rama.[75]

The Rebbe also says that this halacha applies to all three *tefillos, Shacharis, Minchah,* and *Maariv.* The only difference is that more time should be spent on this preparation before *Shacharis* than before the other *tefillos*.[76]

To summarize:

---

73. פי"א.
74. ראה לדוגמא אג"ק חי"ח ע' קכז.
75. ראה אג"ק חי"א ע' שפ.
76. אג"ק חי"ח ע' קנג. חי"א ע' רל.

1. Before beginning to daven, you should consider as if you are in the *Beis Hamikdash,* and you should think that you are speaking directly to Hashem Himself.
2. You should also tell yourself: If I would be speaking to a king of flesh and blood I would be extremely careful with every word I say; how much more so should I be careful when speaking to Hashem with my every word and thought, because Hashem hears my thoughts as well. (Additionally, you should realize that since davening is important for you both spiritually and physically, you certainly have the ability to remove all distracting thoughts.)
3. You should spend some time before davening thinking about Hashem's infinite greatness. For example, reflect on the idea that the entire universe consists of merely a single thought of Hashem that He is projecting into existence out of nothingness, and that He is the only true existence. Compared to the real truth of Hashem's existence, all worldly matters are utterly futile and the only thing that matters is Hashem and His mission for us. (This thought process should include the beginning of Tanya Chapter 41.)

These ideas should be contemplated upon before davening; during davening, you should focus on thinking the meaning of the words you are saying.

These ideas—namely, what it means to think about Hashem's greatness, how to remove worldly desires from your heart, and so on—are explained in Chassidus at length. This is why it is important to think Chassidus before davening every day (as explained in Section 3).

Some More Practical Tips

Not all of these tips are mentioned in Halacha, but they seem to work well:

1. It's important to relax completely before davening; to simply sit down, relax, and allow your thoughts to gather.[77] You should remain serious but also be relaxed, to ensure that davening is something natural and enjoyable and not a burden *chas veshalom.*

2. When saying the words, it's important to take up a pace that works for you, one that is not too fast nor too slow.

3. It's very helpful to have a tune to use for davening (either a *nigun* or a simple personal tune). This way, it's as if you are singing the words of davening and not just reciting them monotonously.

4. The Shulchan Aruch states that the words must be said loud enough for you yourself to hear,[78] but it doesn't have to be louder than that. Depending on how you feel, you may prefer to daven quietly or out loud, whichever way helps you concentrate better.

5. If you are familiar with the Hebrew words, you can sometimes look at the English translation while saying them to make it easier to think their meaning. Obviously, it's preferable to look inside the siddur while saying the words. But since it's hard to avoid getting distracted at times, if you feel that it's getting hard to concentrate while looking at the actual Hebrew words, you can look at the English translation to make it easier.

---

77. See above, "Removing Distractions."

78. או"ח סי' קא.

6. When you are trying to think the meaning of a word, it can help to picture the meaning of the word (in English) in your mind while saying it.

7. If you said words without *kavanah,* you should not repeat them in order to have *kavanah* (except for those places where *kavanah* is *me'akav,* as explained in Chapter 1). Instead, you should think over the meaning of the words you just said and then continue.[79]

---

79. ראה כתר שם טוב שבהערה 58.
וראה גם מאמרי אדה"ז הקצרים ע' תקפ"א: "אם בא לאדם איזה בלבול במחשבתו בתפילתו הוא מהלב והוא כמו אדם אחד שמדבר עמו בעת תפילתו כך הלב הוא כמו אדם אחר ממש רוח הבהמיות כי האדם הוא מורכב ומבלבל מחשבתו שבמוחו. אמנם אעפ"י שאמר קצת דברים שלא במחשבת הלב לא יחזור לראש אם לא במקום שאחז"ל בפסוק ראשון דק"ש ובאבות אבל לא במקומות אחרים. והטעם שמעתי כי א"צ לאדם כ"א לדבר כ"ב אותיות במחשבה והיא הנשמה שמחי' את כל אותיות תפילתו כמשל אדם גדול כמו עוג מלך הבשן מחייהו נשמה קטנה של תנוק קטן בן יומו כך המחשבה מחי' את הדבור".

Chapter 5.
KAVANAH WHEN SAYING HASHEM'S NAMES AND THE FIRST POSSUK OF SHEMA

❧ Hashem's Names

Halacha specifies certain *kavanos* you should concentrate on each time you say Hashem's Name.[80]

When saying the Name of Hashem that is spelled *Yud Kei Vov Kei* and pronounced *Ad-n-y*, you should think that *Yud Kei Vov Kei* signifies that Hashem is *Hayah, Hoveh, VeYiyihiyeh*, meaning that Hashem has existed, exists, and will exist forever. In addition, you should think the meaning of the Name as it's pronounced (*Ad-n-y*), namely, that Hashem is the absolute Master of all.

When saying the Name of Hashem as it is spelled *Alef Daled Nun Yud*, you should think that Hashem is the absolute Master of all.

When saying the Name *Elokim* (or a name derived from *Elokim*, such as *Elokeinu*), you should think that Hashem is All-Powerful and that He has the ability to do whatever He desires in both the higher and lower spheres (and that all power comes from Him alone and He is the cause of everything[81]).

---

80. שו"ע או"ח סי' ה.
81. The ideas in parentheses are not mentioned by the Alter Rebbe but are mentioned by other *poskim*.

Being that it is difficult to have all this in mind each time one says Hashem's Name, it is suggested to say a short declaration at the beginning of the day as follows: "Whenever I say the Name *Yud Kei Vov Kei*, I mean that Hashem has existed, exists, and will exist forever, and that he is the absolute Master of all. When I say the Name *Ad-n-y*, I mean that Hashem is the absolute Master of all. And when I say the Name *Elokim*, I mean that Hashem is All-Powerful and that He has the ability to do whatever He desires in both the higher and lower spheres (and that all power comes from Him alone)."[82] However, when saying Hashem's Name in the first *possuk* of *Shema* (where Hashem's name is mentioned three times—"*Hashem Elokeinu Hashem*"), it's better to think these *kavanos* explicitly.[83]

First *Possuk* of *Shema*

There are three ideas one should have in mind when saying שמע ישראל ה' אלקינו ה' אחד. We will first explain these three ideas separately and then how all three ideas join together as one.

1. The oneness of Hashem. When saying "ה' אחד," one should contemplate on the fact that Hashem is the only Ruler over the seven heavens, the earth, the four directions of the globe, and the past, present, and future.[84]

More particularly, the א of אחד indicates that Hashem is the ruler of the world (as the Hebrew word for ruler—*aluf*—is similar to the word *alef*); the ח (eight) indicates that He rules

---

82. סידור תפלה לדוד (לבעל האשל אברהם) סעיף כא. ועיין פסקי תשובות או"ח סי' ה.
83. עיין סידור תפלה לדוד הנ"ל ובביאור הגר"א או"ח סי' ה.
84. שו"ע או"ח סי' סא ס"ו. וראה שער היחוד והאמונה פ"ז.

over the seven heavens and the earth;⁸⁵ and the ד (four) indicates that He rules over the four directions of the globe. And since He is 'ה, meaning that he existed, exists, and will exist forever, His Kingship over the world is also for all time—in the past, present, and future.⁸⁶

2. Hashem's Kingship. When saying *Shema* one should accept *ol malchus shamayim*, that Hashem is our King.⁸⁷

By which word(s) of *Shema* should one concentrate on this idea? It seems that accepting Hashem's Kingship is related to the word אחד:⁸⁸

The Gemara states that the verse *Shema Yisrael* is one of the *pesukei malchiyos* recited during *Musaf* on Rosh Hashanah.⁸⁹ But the word מלך is not mentioned in this *possuk*. How can it be used as one of the *pessukei malchiyos*?

There are two answers to this question.

---

85. Additionally, the letter ח written in *ksav ashuri* has a "roof" on top. This signifies that Hashem is alive (as the letter ח stands for חי, alive) in the summit of the world (see Shulchan Aruch [ibid.], from Menachos 29b).

  Perhaps this *kavanah* complements the general *kavanah* of *echad* (as explained in the text): Hashem transcends the world (the *kavanah* of the "roof" of the *ches*), while at the same time His Kingship permeates all aspects of the world (the general *kavanah* of *echad*). This is similar to the Rebbe's explanation that the word *Oybershter*, which means "the One Above," doesn't tell us who Hashem is, rather that He is beyond any limitation or definition one can provide. Yet, His Essence is known to all, even to children (see Torah Or 14b), because even as He transcends anything and everything, He is found everywhere and rules over every aspect of existence.

86. שו"ע שם, וראה שער היחוד והאמונה שם. וראה ברכות יג, ב: "כיון דאמליכתיה למעלה ולמטה ולארבע רוחות השמים תו לא צריכת", ובפרש"י: "שהארכת שיעור שתחשוב בלבך ה' אחד בשמים ובארץ וד' רוחותיה".

87. ראה ברכות יג, א במשנה: "כדי שיקבל עליו עול מלכות שמים תחלה". וראה שם יג, ב בעניין ק"ש של רבי יהודה הנשיא, ושם יד, ב ואילך.

88. The following discussion is the author's and is inconclusive.

89. ר"ה לב, ב.

1. The Tur[90] explains that Hashem's Kingship is expressed in the word אלקינו, because by saying that He is our G-d, we are accepting Him as our King and that we must fulfill whatever He desires.
2. The Me'iri[91] answers that Hashem's Kingship is connected to the word אחד. Hashem's oneness is such that it excludes any other type of kingship or dominion, as He is the sole ruler over everything.

The Levush[92] quotes both explanations; however, when quoting the Levush, the Alter Rebbe[93] only quotes the explanation that the word אחד demonstrates Hashem's Kingship, and he omits the other explanation (that it is expressed in the word אלקינו). This indicates that the Alter Rebbe follows the Me'iri, and one should concentrate on accepting Hashem's Kingship primarily[94] when saying the word אחד.[95]

To summarize: The main place where we accept Hashem's Kingship is when saying ה' אחד. One should then think that Hashem's oneness is such that He is the only King and that it's impossible for any other kind of kingship to exist, and we should accept Hashem's Kingship upon ourselves to fulfill whatever He desires.[96]

---

90. או"ח סי' קיג.
91. בחידושיו לר"ה שם.
92. או"ח סי' תקצ"א ס"ד.
93. או"ח סי' תקצ"א סי"א.
94. As mentioned earlier (from the Tur), the word אלקינו expresses the acceptance of Hashem's Kingship as well; however, it is expressed *primarily* in the word אחד (see note 96).
95. This also corresponds with the Gemara in *Brachos* (see note 86) that ה' אחד indicates that Hashem rules above, below, and over the four directions of the globe.
96. Perhaps the difference between accepting Hashem's Kingship when saying אלקינו or when saying אחד is as follows: Accepting Hashem as our king because He is *our* G-d (אלקינו) doesn't emphasize that there is no other king other than Him. *Lehavdil*, every country has its king, but he is only the king of that country;

3. Sacrificing one's life for Hashem. When saying *Shema*, one should accept Hashem as his King to the extent that he is prepared to sacrifice his life to fulfill His desire.[97] One should have this *kavanah* when saying the word אחד.[98]

When joining all three ideas together, we can conclude that when saying ה' אחד you should consider the following: I recognize that Hashem is the only ruler and king of the entire universe, and that no power can exist that is separate from Him. I therefore accept His Kingship to fulfill whatever He wishes, even if I must sacrifice my life or personal desires[99] for this purpose.

When a Yid realizes that Hashem is אחד—the only king, creator, guide, and cause of all existence, and that He is the only one who has real importance and is the only true existence (as explained in Tanya Chapter 25), he will accept His Kingship to the point of *mesiras nefesh*, since a Yid is unable to separate himself from His oneness (א איד ניט ער וויל און ניט ער קאן זיין ח"ו א נפרד מאלקות—a Jew is unwilling and unable to become separated from Hashem, *chas veshalom*).[100]

This idea is central to a person's *avodas Hashem* throughout the day. As the Alter Rebbe explains in Tanya,[101] the

---

the citizens of another country have a different king. Whereas by saying that Hashem is our King because He is אחד—the one and only King that exists, we emphasize that we are talking about a different type of kingship altogether—one which is exclusive to Hashem alone, and this is what our acceptance of Hashem's Kingship is really about.

97. ב"ח או"ח ריש סי' סא, הובא במשנה ברורה שם סק"ג.
98. ראה סידור אדה"ז סוף סדר נעילה קודם אמירת שמע ישראל מה שמביא בשם השל"ה שיש לכוון למסור נפשו באחד. וכן מובא בכמה מקומות בדא"ח בנוגע לקריאת שמע של כל יום. וראה לקו"ש ח"ט ע' 12 שמחלק בין זכירת ענין מסירת נפש של כל יום בק"ש (כמבואר בתניא פכ"ה) שהוא רק נתינת כח לקיום תוכ"ץ, ובין עצם ענין מסירת נפש כמו בק"ש של נעילה.
99. מובא בכמה מקומות בדא"ח שהפירוש של מסירת נפש הוא מסירת הרצון, כמו בפסוק "אין נפשי אל העם הזה", שפירוש "נפש" הוא רצון.
100. היום יום כא סיון. וראה ד"ה ועשית ציץ עת"ר ובכ"מ ההפרש בין מסירת נפש של יהודי למס"נ של (להבדיל) אינו-יהודי.
101. פכ"ה.

reason we are commanded to recite *Shema* twice daily is so that we will remember our belief in His oneness to the point of *mesiras nefesh*. This is expressed in everything we do throughout the day, since anything that is against His will is essentially a denial of His true oneness that there is nothing separate from Him, and anything that is in accordance with His Will is an affirmation of His oneness.

This is a deep idea, and it's not always possible to be *ma'arich be'echad* properly by contemplating on it each time you recite *Shema*. Nevertheless, if you think through this concept properly even just once, you can think it over briefly for a minute or less every day when saying *shema*, thus fulfilling the mitzvah properly.

This idea should be thought about while saying the word אחד and afterward, before beginning ברוך שם (as long as he starts doing so within *toch kedai dibur*—about two to three seconds—of saying the word אחד).[102] (This is allowed even *lechatchilah*, as there isn't enough time to think the entire *kavanah* while saying the actual word.)

(See Chapter 3 for further discussion regarding the preferred time to think the meaning of the words of davening—before, while, or after saying the words.)

---

102. ראה שו"ע אדה"ז סי' סא ס"ז.

Chapter 6.
KAVANOS WHEN PERFORMING MITZVOS

In addition to having *kavanah* when davening, it's also important to have at least a basic *kavanah* when doing a mitzvah.

There are two *kavanos* you should have whenever you perform a mitzvah: the general *kavanah*, which applies to all mitzvos equally, and the specific *kavanah* which applies to that particular mitzvah.[103] You should have the general *kavanah* in mind before performing the mitzvah (while saying the *brachah*) and the specific *kavanah* in mind while actually doing the mitzvah.[104]

❦ GENERAL *KAVANAH*

Before performing any mitzvah, be it donning tefillin or tzitzis or reciting *Birchas Hamazon*, you should have in mind that you are fulfilling this mitzvah because Hashem commanded us to do so and in order to bring pleasure and satisfaction to Hashem.

---

103. See *Lekutei Sichos* (Vol. 4, pp. 1191–6) where these two types of *kavanos* are explained and references are given to additional source material.

See also *Lekutei Sichos* (Vol. 13, pp. 41–42) that infusing physicality with holiness through mitzvos is similar to conquering Eretz Yisrael. Accordingly, just as the Yidden spied Eretz Yisrael before entering it, one must think into the (general and specific) meaning of a mitzvah before performing it.

104. אג"ק מוהריי"ץ ח"ח ע' קצז.

Chassidus and Kabbalah add that you should have in mind that you are fulfilling the mitzvah to bring about a *yichud* between *Hakodosh Boruch Hu* and His *shechinah*, i.e., to reveal Hashem within every Jew, and especially within yourself.[105]

(In the *sichos* of 5751–52 the Rebbe mentions that the underlying objective of every mitzvah [and indeed, of every physical activity] is to hasten Moshiach's coming.[106] It follows that it's appropriate to have this in mind as well before performing a mitzvah.)

Specific *Kavanos*

The specific *kavanah* of a mitzvah involves thinking into what this particular mitzvah will accomplish in revealing Hashem within the person and the world at large.

We will explain here the specific *kavanos* of the three mitzvos of tefillin, tzitzis, and sukkah, where having this specific *kavanah* is especially important.[107]

Tefillin. When donning tefillin you should think that through fulfilling this mitzvah you are dedicating your mind and heart to Hashem. This is the specific *kavanah* of tefillin in short; in his siddur,[108] the Alter Rebbe explains what you should think when putting on tefillin in greater detail. The *kavanah* mentioned in the siddur is as follows (with slight additional explanation):

Hashem commanded us to write the tefillin which include four passages from the Torah. These four pas-

---

105. ראה תניא פמ"א וד"ה שמח תשמח תרנ"ז.
106. ראה לדוגמא שיחות ש"פ וירא וש"פ חיי שרה (בעת כינוס השלוחים) תשנ"ב.
107. ראה ב"ח או"ח סי' ח, כה, ותרכה.
108. ע' 12 בסידור תהלת ה'.

sages include two concepts: (1) Hashem's oneness, and (2) that Hashem took us out of Mitzrayim. (The passage of *Shema* discusses Hashem's oneness, that ה׳ אחד—Hashem is the only true existence, while the passages of *Kadesh* and *Vehayah Ki Yevi'acha* mention that Hashem took us out of Mitzrayim.)

Hashem wants us to think about these two ideas so that we will remember the miracles and wonders He performed for us. These miracles demonstrate (1) that He is the only Creator and controls everything, and (2) that He has the ability to do as He desires both above and below.

Hashem commanded us to don the tefillin on the arm next to the heart and on the head near the brain, so that we will dedicate the soul which is in the brain (i.e., the *nefesh ha'elokis*) and the desires and thoughts of the heart (i.e., the *nefesh habahamis*) to His service. Thus, by putting on tefillin one will think about the Creator and diminish the pursuit of physical pleasures, because he will endeavor to dedicate his life to the mission given to him by Hashem.

Chassidus and Kabbalah add that one should have in mind before putting on tefillin that this mitzvah will draw down from Hashem's *chochmah* and *binah* (the levels of *chochmah* and *binah* of *Atzilus*)—which correspond to the *parshiyos* of *Kadesh* and *Vehayah Ki Yevi'acha*—into his own intellect; and it will draw down love and fear of Hashem—which correspond to the *parshiyos* of *Shema* and *Vehayah Im Shamo'a*—into his own heart.[109]

To explain this *kavanah* in more practical terms:

---

109. תניא ריש פמ״א.

By putting on tefillin a person connects his intellect—i.e., his ability to think and understand—with Hashem's "intellect," and he connects his feelings and emotions with Hashem's "emotions."

This connection is different than the connection of one's intellect to Hashem through learning Torah and the connection of one's emotions to Hashem when davening. The connection through learning is by actually filling one's mind with the understanding of Hashem's Wisdom, and the connection while davening is by actually becoming aroused with love and fear of Hashem. By putting on tefillin, however, you don't understand or feel anything; all you did was the action of putting them on. But this itself connects your mind to Hashem in such a way that Hashem's "intellect" can become the way you will think, so that the holiness of the Torah will be able to permeate your mind, and it connects your emotions to Hashem in such a way that Hashem's "emotions" can become the way you will feel, so that love and fear of Hashem will be able to enter your heart.[110]

Tzitzis. When putting on tzitzis (or a tallis) you should have in mind that by looking at the tzitzis we can remember all of the mitzvos of Hashem (because the 8 strings, 5 knots, and *gematria* of tzitzis—600—add up to 613), and this will remind us to do what Hashem desires and not stray after our *yetzer hara*.[111] According to Chassidus and Kabbalah you should also think that by wearing tzitzis we draw Hashem's Kingship upon ourselves, meaning that we accepts Hashem as our king.[112]

---

110. ראה ד"ה איתא במדרש תהלים תרנ"ג (המאמר לבר מצוה). וראה גם ד"ה את הוי' האמרת תש"ל.
111. סידור אדה"ז (ע' 11 בסידור תהלת ה').
112. ראה תניא פמ"א.

Sukkah. When sitting in the sukkah you should have in mind that by dwelling in the sukkah we remember how Hashem provided us with the *ananei hakavod* (as well as with actual booths) when He took us out of Mitzrayim, and that He takes care of us and provides for our needs now as well.[113]

---

113. שו"ע או"ח סי' תרכה.

Chapter 7.
THE *CHASSIDISHE PIRUSH HAMILOS*

In addition to thinking the simple meaning of the words of davening, you can expand your understanding of the *tefillos* by studying their order and the significance of the sentences and words. This will help you develop a feeling for what you are saying.

On a basic level, you can study *My Prayer* (Kehos, authored by R. Nissen Mindel) or similar books that explain the background and underlying meaning of the *tefillos*. If you are comfortable with Hebrew, you can study *sefarim* such as Avudraham and Otzar HaTefillos, or you can learn the explanations of Rashi, Metzudos, Radak, and other *mefarshim* relating to the sections of davening found in Tehillim.[114] Eventually you can move on to more advanced explanations.

On a deeper level, you should also learn the *chassidishe* meaning of the words. There are two ways to do this. One way is a *derech ketzarah va'aruchah*—a shorter way that's ultimately longer, and the second way is a *derech aruchah u'ketzarah*—a longer way that's ultimately shorter. The first way is to study the *likuttim* that present short explanations and ideas from Chassidus on davening, such as Siddur Lekutei Torah (Hebrew), the Illuminated by Chassidus siddur (English), and similar *sefarim*. The second way is to study Siddur Im Dach, the original *maamarim* quoted in the *likuttim*, and so on. Although learning an entire *maamar* to develop a

---

114. ראה ספר השיחות תש"ו-ה'שי"ת ע' 8.

feeling for a small section of davening will take much longer, this method is obviously much more effective.

The ideal way to increase your knowledge of the *chassidishe pirush hamilos* is by having a *seder* to study Siddur Im Dach or other *maamarim* that will help you develop a deeper appreciation for the various parts of davening. This can take many years to do properly, but after all, davening is an *avodah* that will continue for your entire life, and after learning a few of these *maamarim* you will begin to enjoy davening much more. Additionally, when you learn a *maamar* that contains an explanation of a part of davening (as many *maamarim* do), you can think over that idea when reaching that part of davening and try to feel how this is the deeper meaning of the words.

Section 3:
THINKING CHASSIDUS

This section will offer practical guidance on how to think Chassidus. But first, we must explain the significance of thinking Chassidus and what it accomplishes, as well as a number of relevant important concepts you must be aware of before beginning to work on thinking Chassidus. These introductions comprise the first five chapters of this section.

The first chapter will provide some background on the concept of working on yourself to think about Hashem and achieve a Divine perspective on reality (עבודה פנימית בהמוח והלב), starting with the Chovos HaLevavos and the Rambam and continuing with how this idea is applied in Tanya and in Chassidus in general. This background should serve as the basis for realizing the fundamental importance of thinking Chassidus as the best method possible of fulfilling the mitzvos of being aware of Hashem and loving and fearing Him. These mitzvos are essential to Yiddishkeit, permeating and giving energy to every aspect of the life of a Yid, and they are of no less importance than other mitzvos such as tefillin and Shabbos.

The second, third, and fourth chapters will explain how you can and should let Chassidus affect you on the deepest and most personal level of your being, which will inspire you with true joy from the fact that you possess a deep, internal connection with Hashem.

The fifth chapter will provide some basic guidelines on how to look at Chassidus as an extremely deep and profound knowledge as well as something very practical that can be applied to your daily life.

It's important to point out that you shouldn't wait until you finish mastering the *pirush hamilos* of the entire davening before beginning to think Chassidus. This is because as much as it is important to know what we are saying, it is of equal importance—or perhaps of even more importance—to know to Whom we are talking. This can only be accomplished by thinking about Hashem as it is explained in Chassidus, which enables us to understand the truth and greatness of Hashem and how we can find Him in our lives, especially when we daven to Him.

Chapter 1.
TRANSFORMING ONE'S PERSPECTIVE[115]

୧୧ All in the Mind

Before approaching the idea of thinking Chassidus, it is important to realize that studying Chassidus is not just one of many things a chossid does; rather, it is supposed to transform a person's outlook and introduce a G-dly perspective.

In today's world there are many books that are classified as "self-help." Many of these books are based on the understanding that our actions result from the mind and that by improving our outlook our behavior will change.

These books show how to improve life through developing a proper perspective of yourself, building proper relationships, dealing with problems, and so on. This principle—that by changing your perspective you can introduce vast improvements in your life—is something even many non-religious individuals adhere to.

However, for a Yid who sees everything in the context of the Torah's teachings, the process of changing your perspective in the right direction takes place on a completely different level, and it achieves far greater results.[116]

---

115. This chapter originally appeared as an article in the Perspectives magazine, Nissan 5775. My thanks to R. Shimon Hellinger and his staff (and to R. Eli Leib Rubin) for helping prepare the article, which appears here with slight adaptations.

116. In many of the Rebbe's *sichos* he explains that all of the mitzvos in the Torah—even those that make sense logically—should be fulfilled only because Hashem

To help understand how this works, this chapter will outline how this idea was explained in classical Jewish works and how it is explained in Chassidus.

A Torah Mindset

R. Bechaye Ibn Pekuda lived in Saragossa, Spain, during the generation that preceded the Rambam. He wrote a *sefer* called Chovos HaLevavos. In the *sefer's* introduction he writes that until his time there were many *sefarim* explaining how to fulfill the mitzvos that are performed with the body, but none that explained how to fulfill the mitzvos that are performed in the mind and heart. These are the "duties of the heart" after which his *sefer* was titled. He argues that these duties are of equal or greater importance than the duties of the body and are deserving of as much explanation. While simple belief in the tradition may be sufficient for children and the ignorant, it does not suffice for intelligent individuals.

Nearly a thousand years later, the *sefer* is still considered a basic *sefer* of *avodas Hashem* in all Jewish circles.

Besides for raising awareness about the importance of the duties of the heart, R. Bechaye Ibn Pekuda also made deep philosophical, ethical, and theological ideas accessible to the common man. Up until that point, only great scholars were able to discern how to carry out these ideas. But his *sefer* was

---

commanded us to do them. This concept requires a person to take a deeper look at many of the things he does. For example, when someone pays his workers on time or gives tzedakah, he doesn't do so (only) because he understands that it's a good thing to do, but because Hashem commanded him to do so. In a similar sense, we must take a deeper look at the concept of focusing our thoughts and changing our perspective. A Yid knows that he is commanded by Hashem to think the right things and realizes that's it much deeper than just self-help. Through focusing his thoughts the way Hashem wants him to, he creates a connection to Hashem within his mind and heart.

written in the colloquial Arabic and explained in clear terms what it means to serve Hashem with the heart and how to go about accomplishing this. These explanations also addressed fundamental Jewish beliefs such as the oneness of Hashem, *hashgachah pratis*, and trust in Him. The goal of these explanations was not only to give a person more instructions (as in Halacha, which tells a person what is permitted and what is forbidden), but also to give a person new perspectives on how to look at Hashem and our relationship with Him.

For example: In many places *Chazal* describe the destructiveness of arrogance and how it is forbidden just like idol worship.[117] However, they do not clearly explain *how* one can remove arrogance and attain humility. However, in the Gate of Humility[118] R. Bechaye lists seven reflections[119] to consider in order to rid oneself of arrogance. They can be summarized as four themes:

1. **Physical insignificance and inadequacy.** The physical body is created from lowly physical elements. Even if someone is physically comfortable, life is short, passes quickly, and is replete with problems of which he cannot free himself.

2. **Spiritual inadequacy.** However hard one tries, no one is perfect, and every person must acknowledge that he comes very short from fulfilling everything he should in Torah and mitzvos. When the Day of Judgment comes, no excuses will be accepted.

3. **The all-encompassing greatness of Hashem.** Being constantly in the presence of Hashem should inspire tremendous awe. The sages of old were so great that

---

117. See, for example, Sotah 4b.
118. Gate 6, Chapter 5.
119. The Rebbe would translate *lehisbonein* as "to reflect upon."

among them were people like R. Yonasan ben Uziel whose words of Torah would consume a bird flying overhead. These sages were on a lower level than the prophets of old (the *nevi'im*). Yet, the *nevi'im* (like Daniel) were terrified in the presence of angels. The angels, in turn, are terrified in the presence of Hashem. Certainly we, who are on an incomparably lower level than all of them, should be even more awestruck by the fact that we are constantly in Hashem's presence.

4. **The stature of the individual in comparison to Hashem.** All of mankind and the entire world is created with Hashem's infinite wisdom. When a person considers himself in comparison to all of mankind, he is extremely small indeed. How much more so is this the case in comparison to the entire Planet Earth, and even more so in comparison to the entire universe. One cannot begin to imagine how small he is in comparison to the Creator of everything, before whom a person is viewed as non-existent.

These ideas are not just facts to be learned and stored away. They are ways of training our brains *how* to think about ourselves and our purpose. In other words, these lessons provide us with life-tools, not just with static information.

A Halachic Obligation

The Rambam took this principle and made it clear that Halacha regards these mitzvos as the foundations of the entire Torah.

The Rambam's *sefer* is comprised of *"halachos halachos"*—it is entirely dedicated to Halacha. And the Rambam placed the theological fundamentals of Torah at the very beginning of this work. The first volume is *Sefer Hamada*, the Book of Knowledge, so named because it explains the mitzvos that are performed in the mind and heart. The reason these mitzvos come first is because they are a prerequisite for the proper fulfillment of the other mitzvos.

The first section in this volume is *Hilchos Yesodei HaTorah*, the Laws of [the mitzvos which are] the Foundations of the Torah, in which the Rambam explains the first four mitzvos: (1) To know (i.e., to understand[120]) the existence of Hashem. (2) To know (i.e., to understand) the oneness of Hashem. (3) To love Hashem. (4) To fear Hashem. The Rambam begins this section by saying, "The ultimate foundation for the fulfillment of the Torah and mitzvos and of all wisdom is to know and understand that Hashem is the first existence Who is constantly bringing everything else into existence."

After explaining these and a few other fundamental mitzvos, the Rambam proceeds with *Hilchos Deios*, the Laws of Attitudes. Here he explains how we connect to Hashem by shaping our attitudes according to the way He wants. Hashem wants us to have a generous attitude, a positive attitude, a merciful one, a well-balanced one and so forth. This process of shaping our attitudes is almost entirely fulfilled through focusing our thoughts properly on what is explained in the Torah.

---

120. In the beginning of *Mitzvas Haamanas Elokus* (in *Derech Mitzvosecha*) the Tzemach Tzedek explains that when the Rambam says that the mitzvah is to "know," he doesn't just mean to *believe* that Hashem exists and is the Creator. As the Semag asks, "If one doesn't believe that Hashem exists, how can he accept a commandment to believe?" Rather, it means that after one believes in the existence of Hashem, he should reflect upon His true existence and how it transcends (and permeates) all other types of existence.

Similarly, the way to fulfill the mitzvos of knowing His oneness and of loving and fearing Him are attained through focusing our minds and contemplating on His oneness, greatness, and so on.

Another example: One of the mitzvos he explains is the mitzvah to love every Yid like one loves himself. This mitzvah is not fulfilled simply by giving tzedakah, and it is not violated only by physically hurting another. It is fulfilled by thinking good about another Yid until you *want* to help them, and it is transgressed by thinking bad about another Yid until opposite feelings are aroused (*"Lo sisna es achicha bilvavecha,"* "Do not hate your brother in your heart"). This is another example of how the Rambam codified the concept of focusing our thoughts properly as part of Halacha.

A Chassidic Mindset

All of this is the way this idea was explained in classic Jewish texts that have existed for close to a thousand years. But Chassidus takes it all a step further.

In Tanya the Alter Rebbe defines our service of Hashem in the context of the struggle between the *nefesh ha'elokis* and the *nefesh habahamis.* In Chapter Twelve he describes the model of service of Hashem that we should strive for as being that of the *beinoni*. The *beinoni* makes sure that his *nefesh ha'elokis* is always in control of how he thinks, speaks, and acts. How does the *beinoni* always have the ability to control his actions? Because Hashem created man with the innate ability for the mind to control the heart. In other words, if you know what the right thing is, you can do it even if you don't feel like it, whether it's in deed, speech, or even thought.

The innovation here is that the Alter Rebbe is not simply giving you tools to train your behavior, but tools to train and transform your inner self, your intellect and your emotions. This is not simply about self-control, but about a methodological process of internal transformation. This principle is encapsulated in the phrase *"moach shalit al haleiv,"* "the mind controls the heart." This control can be extended in two different ways:[121]

1. The more basic level is that the mind controls the way you act upon your emotions. A person's actions flow directly from his emotions. You do what you feel like unless your mind tells you otherwise. This is the most basic idea of self-discipline, to train yourself to act a certain way despite your natural tendencies and desires. This is how a child learns to behave like a *mentsch* and how a Yid learns to behave like a Yid. Here, when we say "the mind controls the heart," we mean that it controls the way your emotions impact your behavior. (In Chassidic lexicon this idea is called *iskafya*—see Tanya Chapter 13.)

   This does not mean that the mind is simply controlling your behavior and bypassing the heart. The heart itself must also be affected; you must *want* to do what's right and overcome conflicting feelings because you know that this is the right thing to do. Intellectually knowing what's right won't change your behavior unless you have some kind of emotional desire in your heart to do the right thing.

---

121. See *hemshech* Rosh Hashana 5663 and 5665, where the Rebbe Rashab elaborates on three concepts in the development of character. One is in the form of *mutba*, the natural potential for emotions, where one's actions are only a function of *NeHY* (actions without strong feeling). The second is *murgash*, actual felt emotions, where one's actions are a function of *ChaGaS* (natural emotions that are revealed and channeled through the mind). The third form is *muskal*, intellectually developed emotions, where one's actions are a function of *ChaBaD* (profound and penetrating understanding).

   He explains further that on the level of *murgash*, the mind reveals the natural emotions and harnesses them so that a person will exercise self-control and act based on what he knows is right despite his emotions. On the level of *muskal*, the depth of the mind elevates the emotions to the level of intellect, so that a person's feelings will match the way he thinks. This is the idea of *is'hapcha*.

2. A deeper level of the control of the mind over the heart is that the mind *transforms* the desires of the heart to *truly* want what's right. (In Chassidic lexicon this is termed *is'hapcha*—see the *maamar* Basi Legani 5715.) This process starts at the age of Bar Mitzvah, when a person has enough *daas* to truly internalize ideas and let them affect his heart. Through constantly working on davening and *hisbonenus,* you can actually change how you feel about things and experience ever deeper levels of connection to Hashem.

Chovos HaLevavos can bring a person to a certain level of this transformation, but a true transformation can only happen through Chassidus. This is because Chassidus is the revelation of G-dly knowledge and reveals the inner dimensions of the *neshamah* that have this transformative power. Ideas based on human intellect, by contrast, cannot accomplish the same degree of transformation (see the *hakdamah* of Tanya).

This also explains why there is such a deep distinction between what a Yid can achieve and, *lehavdil,* what a *goy* can achieve (See Tanya Chapter 1). When a Yid uses the intellect of the *nefesh ha'elokis,* he can always control the emotions of the *nefesh habahamis* and not allow them to express themselves in action. This ability is not just because Hashem created every human with the ability for the mind to control the heart. In the case of a *goy,* both his intellect and emotions are created beings and derive from the same spiritual level *(kelipas noga* or *shalosh klipos hatemei'os).* It's just that the mind is superior and more powerful than the heart and can therefore control it.[122]

In the case of a Yid, however, his *nefesh ha'elokis* reveals Hashem—it's saying the truth, and his *nefesh habahamis* conceals Hashem—it's expressing falsehood, and falsehood compared to truth has no reality, just as darkness is automatically dispelled by light. A Yid has a *nefesh ha'elokis* that is bound up with Hashem to the point that this connection is his entire life. He is willing to give up his life rather than separate himself from Hashem by going against His will. The connection of the *nefesh ha'elokis* to Hashem isn't because he figured out that Hashem is the best thing for his existence; it comes from the *neshamah* "seeing" and being intrinsically bound with the truth of Hashem. This awareness of His truth drives the *neshamah* to reunite with its source even though it will lose its independent existence as a result (see Tanya Chapters 18 and 19). And since this connection is so strong and transcends any logic (even the logical motive of self-preservation), he will do anything to connect himself to Hashem through Torah and mitzvos. Every Yid can focus on this basic concept at any time, enabling him to control his actions, as explained in the fourteenth chapter of Tanya.

There is a general principle that *ain chavush matir es atzmoi*, a prisoner can't free himself, and only someone from without can let him out. Similarly, the limitations of human intellect and emotions can't be completely transcended through human intellect. However smart someone is, he can't transcend being human. Only Hashem, who transcends any and all limitations, can give us a way to grow beyond our human limitations. This is why the wisdom of even the greatest

---

122. See Tanya Chapter 51 that the vitality of the soul is revealed within the rest of the body—including the heart—through the brain, and that's why the brain can control the heart.

Torah scholars—if their teachings were based on human understanding—doesn't have the power to effect such a transformation. Only the teaching of *pnimiyus hatorah*—especially the teachings of Chassidus—have the ability to bring about that transformation, since they are a revelation of Divine Intellect. Divine Intellect is the source of human intellect and has the ability to change it (just as a programmer can change the computer program from the outside, but the program can't change itself from within). Only through contemplating on the Divine Wisdom of *pnimiyus hatorah* can a person achieve real transformation of the mind and heart and reach a different type of awareness of Hashem.

The Process of Reflection

Accordingly, attaining a greater awareness of Hashem is not only one mitzvah, or many mitzvos, or even many fundamental mitzvos. It is a process through which we are able to serve Hashem at any second of the day. This concept is further brought out in Tanya Chapter 42. The Alter Rebbe explains that if someone will spend time every day to reflect on the fact that Hashem is watching him at every moment, he will able to control himself at any time by reminding himself of this idea for even just a few moments. The ability to focus our thoughts on Hashem is thus not only a foundation behind our service of Hashem, but it is the constant force pulling us through all of the different situations throughout the day.

Even *kabbalos ol*, which means to accept Hashem as our King without understanding, is something that happens primarily in the mind. It means that a person consciously resolves with complete certainty to do whatever Hashem wants, no matter what.

The idea that the mind can control the heart is not an innovation of Chassidus, as we demonstrated above from the Chovos HaLevavos and the Rambam. The innovation of Chassidus is that we can use our mind to understand and connect to G-dly ideas that are essentially higher than human intellect, applying them as the basis of our conduct in our daily lives.

An example of this—a G-dly idea Chassidus explains in a way that the human intellect can understand and channel into action—is the first contemplation presented in Tanya as a way to reveal our hidden love for Hashem (see Chapter 18 and onward at length, and briefly in Chapter 14). To understand Hashem's oneness as meaning that He is the only existence *(yichuda ilaa)* is something no human being can ever attain alone; it is a revelation of *Elokus*—a Divine perspective. Yet not only can a Yid understand this concept, he can connect to it to such an extent that it can drive him to actual self-sacrifice, to the point that he is willing to give up his life rather than deny Hashem's oneness. When we understand our connection to Hashem based on that higher level, we can bring that depth into our daily lives.

Although we are incapable of living with *yichuda ilaa* on a day-to-day basis, being aware of the idea can nevertheless impact us.

In *Kuntres Eitz HaChaim* the Rebbe Rashab explains that our primary service of Hashem should be with *yichuda tataa*—an awareness of Hashem as the one who is creating and giving life to the world. However, in order for our *avodas Hashem* to be as it should, it must be permeated with a higher awareness that there is no existence at all other than Him. Without this recognition, our ego is still present and blocks out the true oneness of Hashem. It is only when a Yid knows that in reality there is nothing other than Him that all of his actions can become channels to reveal the true oneness of Hashem, which is the purpose of all of creation (see Tanya Chapter 33).

This type of awareness is something that only Chassidus, a revelation of divine perspective rather than human intellect, can generate.

In addition to having an effect on our daily service of Hashem, this realization can have a deep long-term effect and be the determining factor that will steer us in the right direction. In Tanya Chapter 12 the Alter Rebbe explains that when a Yid evokes a love and fear of Hashem through reflecting on His greatness during davening, it leaves an impression on him that lasts the entire day. In other words, when a person will realize that what he really cares about is Hashem and nothing else, when he will be confronted by a difficult situation during the day, he will have already attained the right attitude and know instinctively how to deal with it. He won't have to struggle as much to focus on doing what's right, since he is already connected to a higher perspective due to his mindfulness during the morning davening.

Thus, thinking Chassidus and reflecting on the ideas it explains plays a significant role in creating G-dly perspectives and transforming a person's mindset. This will affect his daily life in a real way and change the dynamics of his relationship both with Hashem and with others.

From all of the above it should be clear that thinking Chassidus and creating a G-dly perspective is not a *chassidishe minhag*; it's not a custom of sorts reserved only for great chassidim. Every Yid has the merit and responsibility to develop a real and meaningful awareness of Hashem, just as he has the merit and responsibility to put on tefillin and keep Shabbos. Hashem in his great kindness has given us the treasure of Chassidus, enabling each and every one of us to develop an awareness of Hashem in an incredibly deep and enjoyable manner, and every Yid has the ability to make use of this gift by working on his mind and heart.[123]

---

123. The following real-life story serves as an example of how applying Chassidus to one's life is within the reach of every person (see *Hamashpia: R. Shlomo Chaim Kesselman*, pp. 299–300; 318–319).

R. Bentzion Cohen *sheyichyeh* was born in America to unobservant parents. After arriving in Eretz Yisroel and coming closer to Yiddishkeit, he went to learn in the Lubavitcher Yeshiva in Kfar Chabad, where he was taught how to put on *tefillin* and daven every day.

Bentzion noticed certain *bochurim* who would sit silently before davening every day for ten minutes, and he wondered what they were doing. Someone told him they were involved in *hisbonenus*, reflection on ideas of Chassidus. When he asked how this was done, he was directed to R. Shlomo Chaim Kesselman, the *mashpia* of the yeshiva at the time, who guided him how to think Chassidus before davening and throughout the day.

After some time, Bentzion was thinking Chassidus for ten to fifteen minutes before davening every day, and R. Shlomo Chaim mentioned this to the Rebbe at a *yechidus*. The Rebbe was very pleased by this piece of news. Standing up from his chair, he said, "If only all the *bochurim* would think Chassidus for five or ten minutes before davening!"

This is an example of someone who did not have a Chassidic (or religious) background, yet he recognized the important role of thinking Chassidus in his personal life, until he became a model for others to learn from.

Chapter 2.
SEARCHING FOR *ELOKUS*

The Rebbe Rashab explains that in order for a person to receive and benefit from what can be accomplished by thinking Chassidus, he must first be a *keili* for it. To be a true *keili*, one must experience a true arousal to turn to Hashem (התעוררות תשובה אמיתית) and be truly searching for *elokus*.[124]

What this means is that Chassidus will only truly affect you if you are searching. Someone who thinks he is fine hasn't opened himself up to allow Chassidus to penetrate him. You must realize that you are missing something, and you must truly feel a need to connect to Hashem. When you feel such a need and then think Chassidus properly, it will revive you and give you *chayus*, as it will be providing you with what you are lacking.

This doesn't mean that you shouldn't think Chassidus until you do complete *teshuvah*; to the contrary, the fact that you are thinking about Hashem will help you do *teshuvah*. What it does mean is that you should recognize that you must be searching for something and have a goal of becoming closer to Hashem, and then thinking Chassidus will help you.

You shouldn't think Chassidus just because it says in *sefarim* that it's a good idea or for some other reason (because your *mashpia* told you to do so or the like). You should think Chassidus because you feel a need to connect to Hashem, to

---

124. *Kuntres HaTefillah*, Chapter 12.

the truth, and to your inner self. It must be done because it's part of who I am and touches the core of my being (נוגע בעצם).

This is unlike action-based mitzvos, where the main thing is the action, and a person's attitude or lack thereof is of secondary importance (relating merely to the revelation of the mitzvah, i.e., how much it will affect him and so on). However, *chovos halevavos*—mitzvos that are situated in the mind and heart—are different. By these mitzvos, a person's attitude, such as his approach to the mitzvah, the reason he is doing it, and so on, plays an important role in the actual mitzvah.

Chapter 3.
TO BE REAL

The Frierdiker Rebbe explains the difference between a shallow person—a *chitzon*, and a deep person—a *pnimi*.[125]

There are two main problems with a *chitzon*. The first problem is that he is a shallow person; he has no depth of personality. He learns, davens, and accomplishes a lot, but he doesn't possess a depth of feeling and appreciation for what he does. A *pnimi*, on the other hand, has a deep concern for what he does; he does things he truly values and thinks into what he does very carefully. A *pnimi* makes sure that something that truly matters is done properly. When a *pnimi* learns Chassidus, he thinks about what he learns until he truly understands it. When he continues on to davening, he thinks over the idea he has learnt until he actually feels it. He takes his time with what he does and doesn't rush things through, and he knows that he must do a proper job. This is especially true in *avodas Hashem*. He makes sure he understands what he learns, connects to davening, and truly cares about his fellow Yid, which is expressed in the way he helps another. A *chitzon* doesn't have such depth. He does only as much as necessary so he can say that he did what he was supposed to do. When he understands an idea, he understands it superficially and

---

125. לשלימות העניין נביא כאן המ"מ שהם היסודות של הביאור בפנים, עם עוד מ"מ: (א) לקו"ד: ח"א ליקוט ג אותיות ה-ו, ט-י, טז. ח"ב ליקוט טו אותיות ב-ח. ח"ג ליקוט כז אותיות ה-ו. (ב) ד"ה ושבתי בשלום עת"ר ע' עג-עד (במהדורה הישנה). (ג) סה"מ תרס"ג ח"ב, בהביאור של אדמו"ר הריי"ץ על המאמר הראשון של ההמשך, ע' ה-ו.

only as much as necessary, but he doesn't actually grasp the depth of the idea.

The second problem with a *chitzon* is that he isn't honest with himself. Even if he would have the depth of mind to plumb the depths of a difficult piece of Gemara, he doesn't plumb the depths of his own life to find out what he really cares about. A *chitzon* fools himself by thinking that he already understands and feels, that he is doing a satisfactory job, and that he is a good person. He doesn't want to be honest with himself and make sure that he truly understands and cares about Hashem, feels deeply about Hashem, and works diligently on improving himself. A *pnimi*, on the other hand, wants the truth, no matter how hard he will have to work for it. He doesn't fool himself, because he isn't afraid of the truth, what that will demand of him to do, and how much work it will take.

The Rebbe Rashab explains[126] that there are three things necessary for a *chitzon* to become a *pnimi*. First, it must bother him that he is a *chitzon*, that he doesn't really care about the things he should care about. Not that it should bother him that he isn't acting properly, because as we said before, it could be that his performance is exemplary; rather, it should bother him that he is so shallow.

Second, he must have friends who will guide him and ensure that he is proceeding on the correct path to become a *pnimi*. A *chitzon* is used to fooling himself. If he tries to become a *pnimi* without outside help and support, he may fool himself into thinking that he isn't fooling himself when in actuality he *is* fooling himself.

Third, he must make an effort to learn things thoroughly and in depth *(be'iyun)* so that he will grow accustomed to

---

126. ד"ה ושבתי בשלום הנ"ל.

thinking deeply. By getting used to thinking through a *sugya* from beginning to end, he will get used to thinking thoroughly about life in general.[127]

In order for you to approach the idea of thinking Chassidus properly, you must first be aware that this is part of a bigger picture. It is part of your journey to become a *pnimi*, to have real depth of heart and mind and really care about Hashem.

This idea is one of the main concepts discussed in Tanya. The Tanya is based on the *possuk* "*ki karov eilecha,*" "It is extremely close to you in your mouth and *heart* to do [Torah and mitzvos]." How is serving Hashem with real feeling (with one's *heart*) within a person's reach? Because anyone can use his brain to think about whatever he wants, and when he will think about Hashem properly, he will create (or reveal) deep feelings within himself that result from a deep intellectual appreciation of Hashem.[128]

Even if you think Chassidus and don't have an exciting emotional experience, it is still considered as if you are serving Hashem with your heart, because Hashem connects the "positive thought"—the deep contemplation of Chassidus—with the resulting actions, and the appreciation that is felt from that contemplation is also a type of feeling.[129]

---

127. Perhaps the first two pieces of advice are geared at fixing a *chitzon's* second problem (that he isn't honest with himself), while the third piece of advice is directed at the first problem (that he is a shallow person).
128. Tanya, Chapter 17.
129. Tanya, Chapter 16.

Thus, thinking Chassidus is part of your lifelong journey to serve Hashem with real feeling, and this is something you should realize before you begin (סוף מעשה במחשבה תחלה).[130]

---

130. The difference between the idea discussed in Chapter 2 and the idea discussed here can be explained as follows:

The first idea is that a person has to be receptive to Chassidus for it to affect him. Along a similar vein, someone who indulges in eating or similar pleasures won't be sensitive to Chassidus and it won't affect him properly. But while someone who has yet to be complete can overcome that barrier if he works hard (see Tanya Chapter 42 about overcoming the barrier created from *cha"n*), if he has never experienced a true yearning for a deeper connection to Hashem (התעוררות תשובה אמיתית), he has never opened himself up to Chassidus in the first place. Such a person must work on opening himself up so that Chassidus will be able to affect him.

The second idea, however, is that even after a person does open himself up to Chassidus, he must realize what thinking Chassidus is about. He must realize that it is part of his personal journey to serve Hashem with true feeling and become a deep person.

Chapter 4.
ULTIMATE JOY

Learning and contemplating Chassidus is not meant to be a somber experience but a deeply joyful one. This joy is not only the result of the excitement of learning and applying deep ideas, but from the fact that through this process, you reconnect to your essential awareness of Hashem and your connection to Him. This idea is brought out very strongly in Tanya.

In Chapter 33 of Tanya the Alter Rebbe explains that the ultimate joy a person can attain comes from realizing that Hashem is the only true existence, that Hashem is everywhere and is the truth behind everything. He continues to say that this realization itself creates a dwelling place for Hashem in this world. From Hashem's perspective, there is nothing other than Himself; the whole idea of creating a dwelling place for Him is thus an accomplishment from *our* perspective, that *we* should realize and experience the truth of Hashem. That a Yid in this physical world can understand and feel the truth of Hashem's oneness in his physical mind and heart—*this* is what creates a dwelling place for Hashem on the most basic level. (Obviously, this is only the first stage in creating a dwelling place. This awareness and feeling must permeate the world's physical existence as well, not only our own minds and hearts.)

To explain this idea, the Alter Rebbe gives an analogy from a great king who arrived to live in the house of a simple person. One can but imagine the great joy of that simple person for having the honor to host the king. Similarly, when a person understands, feels, and lives with the truth of Hashem's oneness—that there is nothing other than Him, he is actually hosting Hashem, and he should rejoice with all his heart and soul from the fact that Hashem is residing within him.[131] Thus, the greater the awareness a Yid has of Hashem, the greater his joy in being found in His presence, and this joy will continue to grow ever stronger.

In addition to the joy that results from the awareness of Hashem's true oneness and from being constantly found in His presence, a Yid should rejoice from the fact that he can give Hashem pleasure through his *avodah* and through creating a dwelling place for Him.

This joy (both from being found in Hashem's presence and from creating a dwelling place for Hashem) is so fundamental that the Rebbe included this passage of Tanya as one of the twelve *pesukim*. What's more, he chose this to be the final *possuk*, and as *Chazal* say, "Hakol holech achar hachisum," i.e., the end of something expresses the entire thing. This emphasizes that the ultimate goal is to allow Hashem's genuine joy in us to be manifest within ourselves and the entire world. This, in turn, is accomplished when we rejoice in Him and His oneness, as is explained in Chassidus.

Thus, the purpose of thinking Chassidus isn't only to provide us with more depth in the service of Hashem, but also to create an awareness that we are found in Hashem's presence, to live with the truth that Hashem is the only existence, and to rejoice in this constantly. The goal isn't to become more

---

131. This is expressed in the *possuk* we say daily during davening (in *Hodu*): "Oz vichedvah bimkomo," "Strength and joy are in His presence."

serious and somber, but to live a higher life, to rejoice in the truth even though we can't see it with our physical eyes.

Being connected to a higher type of life experience in this manner will inevitably prevent a person from stumbling in his life experience as it exists down below. R. Meir of Premishlan was able to walk up and down an icy hill without slipping because he was connected to above.[132] Similarly, through being connected to above by thinking Chassidus and becoming aware of Hashem's truth, we will undoubtedly have the power to make it through the icy hill of life.

---

132. לקו"ד ליקוט טו אות ג.

Chapter 5.
PROFOUND AND PRACTICAL

There are two additional ideas related to learning Chassidus that should be explained before we elaborate on the practical aspects of thinking Chassidus.

The first idea is to remove ideas from their materialistic perspective.[133]

There is a fundamental difference between learning *nigleh* and *pnimiyus hatorah*.[134] *Nigleh* discusses physical things that we already know about and can relate to, and all that's needed is for the Torah to come and tell us how we should act with these things. For example, the Torah says that animals that have split hooves and chew their cud may be eaten. We already know what animals are and what it means to have hooves and chew the cud; the Torah just needs to tell us which animals may be eaten and which may not.

Pnimiyus hatorah, on the other hand, discusses spiritual ideas and levels, things we don't know about until we think into them. Take the term *seder hishtalshelus*, which refers to the chainlike order of the spiritual worlds. What makes these worlds have a chainlike order is the fact that each succeeding world receives a lower revelation of *Elokus* and displays less sensitivity to His truth and presence. If someone thinks that the levels of *seder hishtalshelus* are like different floors of a building, and that our physical world is the bottom floor and

---

133. ראה שרש מצות התפלה פ"ב.
134. ראה קונטרס תורת החסידות פי"א ואילך.

an elevator is needed to rise to the top floor of *Atzilus* or *Adam Kadmon,* he is missing the point. All the levels in *seder hishtalshelus* exist simultaneously within our physical space, and to go through *seder hishtalshelus* means to connect to higher levels of spiritual awareness and sensitivity.[135]

From this example we see that to even just figure out what the correct meaning of a term is requires a lot of research and contemplation. This is in addition to discovering what the Torah has to say about *seder hishtalshelus*.[136]

The second idea is what R. Mordechai HaTzaddik quoted from the Baal Shem Tov:[137]

"The *possuk* says, '*Zos hatorah—adam,*' 'This is the Torah—man.' This means that everything in the Torah serves as a lesson for a person."

With regard to Chassidus, this means that everything you learn about in *seder hishtalshelus* must be applied to your *neshamah*. (This is also true the other way around, that you can learn about *seder hishtalshelus* from your *neshamah*. As the *possuk* says, "*Mibsarai echezeh elokah,*" "From my flesh I can see Hashem," meaning that you can learn about Hashem's revelation and presence in the world from the way the *neshamah* is revealed in the body.[138])

For example, if you learn about the concept of *Z'eir Anpin* being drawn down into *Malchus*, you should apply the concept to yourself, namely, that your emotions *(Z'eir Anpin)* should affect your actions *(Malchus)*. The same applies to any concept you learn about in Chassidus.

---

135. ראה לקו"ת פרשת נצבים בביאור לד"ה שוש אשיש דף מח, ד ואילך.
136. See Chapter 6, "Using *Meshalim* to Explain Chassidus," for more on this concept.
137. אג"ק מוהריי"צ ח"ג ס"ע ריט ואילך.
138. ראה קונטרס ענינה של תורת החסידות אות א.

These two ideas illustrate two extremes in learning Chassidus. On the one hand, the concepts discussed in Chassidus describe deep spiritual realities, and you have to think deeper and figure out the real meaning of the terms used. On the other hand, every idea in Chassidus can and should be applied to your personal life and *avodas Hashem*.

Chapter 6.
LEARNING AND THINKING CHASSIDUS

In order for Chassidus to have the proper affect on a person and allow his davening to accomplish what it can accomplish, a certain process must be followed, which includes learning Chassidus and three steps in thinking Chassidus.[139]

❧ Understanding Chassidus

The first step in thinking Chassidus is to think Chassidus when learning it.

This includes two things. First, you must learn Chassidus slowly and carefully and think through the ideas you encounter until you obtain an initial understanding of the material. Second, after completing a session of learning (for example, when finishing to learn Chassidus in the morning), you should think over what you have just learnt until you grasp it properly.

This concept is true regarding all types of learning. Whenever one studies a subject, whether Gemara, Shulchan Aruch, or any other topic, he should think through the concepts while learning, and he must review the ideas again when he finishes. However, this is especially so when it

---

139. אג"ק מוהריי"ץ ח"א ע' רמד ואילך (מובא בהיום יום כ' תמוז). ח"ג ע' תסג ואילך. ע' תקכה ואילך. ח"ח ע' קצט ואילך. וראה גם ד"ה אשר ברא תרח"ץ.

comes to Chassidus which discusses abstract spiritual concepts that can be difficult to grasp.

Ideally, a person should study with a *chavrusa*. When offering guidance on how to study Chassidus effectively, the Frierdiker Rebbe suggests starting off by choosing *maamarim* that are not so difficult and learning with a *chavrusa* with whom the ideas of the *maamar* can be discussed until they are clear.

When learning with a *chavrusa*, thinking through the ideas when learning can be replaced with a discussion with your *chavrusa*. However, in addition to discussing the *maamar* with a *chavrusa*, you should think over the ideas yourself when finishing a session of learning.[140]

Chassidim say[141] that learning Chassidus consists of thought, speech, and action. The thought of Chassidus refers to thinking over the ideas you have learnt (if learning with a *chavrusa*—after learning, and if learning alone—at the time of learning as well). The speech of Chassidus refers to discussing the ideas with a *chavrusa*. The action of Chassidus refers to writing down the ideas in your own words, i.e., to write a summary of the *maamar* for yourself to see if you have grasped the ideas properly.[142]

Writing down the ideas of the *maamar* isn't always possible and depends on the time and situation (for example, it can't be done on Shabbos and Yom Tov). Similarly, discussing the *maamar* with another is usually limited to learning with a *chavrusa*. However, thinking over the *maamar* is a must in all situations. Of course, it's important to review what you have

---

140. נוסף על האגרות דלעיל, ראה ג"כ ח"ב אגרת שנז.
141. I heard this from R. Nachman Shapiro in the name of elder chassidim.
142. When learning a *hemshech* (such as *Samech Vov* or *Ayin Bais*), you should also write a line explaining the connection of the *maamar* to the previous and subsequent *maamarim* in the *hemshech*.

learnt, but that itself is not sufficient. Even if you have reviewed a *maamar* a few times, you still won't grasp it properly unless you think it over.

Additionally, thinking over what you have learnt enables you to gain even from those topics that are learnt once and not reviewed until much later (like the daily Tanya, weekly Torah Or, and so on) or not reviewed at all (for whatever reason). If these ideas are thought over even once (and certainly if they are thought over more than once), a lasting effect can be gained from them as well.

ANALYZING AND APPRECIATING

The next step, after learning the *maamar* and thinking it over, is to analyze the *maamar* and appreciate its richness and depth.

The Frierdiker Rebbe explains this concept with a *mashal* from how Gemara is studied.

When a person studies Gemara, he must first learn it and understand it properly. He must also think it over to make sure he understands it, as explained above. After thinking over what he has learnt, he can begin analyzing the *sugya* at greater depth. He can consider the advantages in the logic of each opinion and the novelty of each point in the Gemara. By analyzing the *sugya*, he can enjoy the richness and depth of each point and derive great satisfaction from this knowledge. (Analyzing a *sugya* in such a way requires a sharp mind, and it cannot be done by every person.)

All this similarly applies to thinking Chassidus. The first step is to think over what you have learnt to make sure you understand it properly. The next step is to think it over again, this time focusing on analyzing and comparing the ideas and appreciating their novelty and richness.

When analyzing a *maamar*, there are two ideas that are helpful to keep in mind.

The first idea is to think through the *seder* of the *maamar*. Think over the questions and the answers, and see how the points of the *maamar* flow from one to the next and build up upon each other.

The second idea is to think through the *meshalim* given in the *maamar* and consider the ideas they are trying to express, as explained in the following section.

Using *Meshalim* to Explain Chassidus

The use of *meshalim* plays an important role in explaining Chassidus to yourself. Chassidus discusses ideas that relate to spiritual truths and levels that cannot be grasped with our physical senses. If something can't be seen, touched, or related to, how can it become a reality? This is where *meshalim* come in. By using a *mashal* from a concept to which we can relate, we can come to relate to the spiritual idea as well.

Since *Chabad Chassidus* explains every spiritual idea with a *mashal*, it is important to know which exact *mashal* is used to explain which spiritual idea. For example, Chassidus often brings a *mashal* from the way the *neshamah* infuses and gives life to the body to explain how Hashem infuses and gives life to the world.[143] (In fact, the Mitteler Rebbe explains in Shaar HaYichud that there is a *mashal* from a person and his soul for every level of the spiritual worlds.) To explain how Hashem's revelation is completely dependent on and nullified to Him, Chassidus often contrasts the way sunlight exists outside of

---

143. See, for example, the *maamar* "Posach Eliyahu" in *Torah Or, Parshas Vayeira*.

the sun to the way it exists within the sun.[144] To explain the nature of our relationship with Hashem, Chassidus cites *meshalim* from the relationship between a child and parent,[145] student and teacher,[146] and subject and king.[147]

These types of *meshalim* are brought in Chassidus in many different ways, and there are many more *meshalim* cited in Chassidus. Whenever a *mashal* is brought, it is important to consider the following questions:

1. What exactly is the *mashal*?
2. Which spiritual idea is the *mashal* coming to explain?
3. How does the *mashal* make this idea clearer and better understood?

If multiple *meshalim* are brought, there are additional questions you should consider:

1. What is the difference between the various *meshalim*?
2. What is the advantage of each one over the other?
3. Why are they all needed?

Sometimes you might think of a *mashal* of your own. In such a case, you should try to figure out if this *mashal* is already brought in Chassidus (perhaps in other words). If it isn't, you should consider: Why isn't it brought down? Perhaps there is a flaw in the *mashal*?

It's very important to remember which *mashal* is used for which idea and not to mix them up. Every detail in Chassidus is exact, and you will only be able to truly understand the

---

144. See, for example, *Shaar Hayichud Veha'emunah*, Chapter 3.
145. See, for example, *Tanya*, Chapter 2 and Chapters 18–25.
146. See, for example, the *maamar Veyadata Moskva*, 5657.
147. See, for example, *Tanya*, Chapters 41f; *Shaar Hayichud Veha'emuna*, beginning of Chapter 7.

ideas it discusses if you have these details organized properly in your mind.

❦ Applying the *Maamar*

The final step in thinking Chassidus is to reflect on the lesson that can be taken from the *maamar* and how it can be applied to one's personal life.

The Frierdiker Rebbe continues to use the *mashal* from learning Gemara to explain this step in thinking Chassidus.

After one has understood the *sugya* and has analyzed each point, he can think over the entire *sugya* once again to figure out the halachic conclusion. At this point he has a totally different kind of focus. He has already applied concentration to understand the Gemara, and he has also experienced the enjoyment in appreciating the depth of the ideas, but now he has an even more serious focus because he knows that this will be relevant to actual practice *(halachah lemaaseh)*. This isn't just an abstract pursuit of knowledge (even of holy knowledge which is a mitzvah to study); the way he understands the *sugya* will be the deciding factor how to perform a mitzvah or avoid transgressing an *issur*. At this point he is completely focused on working out the *maskana* of the *sugya*.

This applies to Chassidus as well. After understanding the ideas, analyzing them, and enjoying their richness, you must think everything over once again and consider what the *maskana* is. You should explain the *bechain*, the "therefore," to yourself: "How can this idea affect me and my conduct, and how can it change my attitude and perspective?"

In particular there are three ideas in this *bechain*:

1. The conclusion that *Elokus* is the best thing in existence.

2. The conclusion that *Elokus* is the best thing for you personally. In other words, not only is it the best thing in existence in general but it is the best thing for you on a personal level.

(Alternatively, the first two ideas can be expressed as follows:
1. The conclusion that Hashem is everywhere and we all exist within Him.
2. The conclusion that Hashem exists where I am right now and I exist within Him.

    In other words, the conclusion must first be that the concept is essentially true, and then you must realize that it is true on a personal level as well.)
3. A reflection on a specific area of conduct that can be improved based on this *maskana*. (This can include the areas of action and speech as well as thought. For example, you can tell yourself, "If I ever find myself in this-and-this situation, I need to approach it the way Chassidus teaches us and not view it the way the *yetzer hara* says is the reality.")

Dividing the Steps

The Frierdiker Rebbe explains that the first step in thinking Chassidus should be done when learning (as explained above), the second step should take place before davening, and the third step should take place during davening.

However, this doesn't mean that you have to go through all three steps each day. As can be easily seen, from when a person learns an idea in Chassidus until it actually affects his actions is a lengthy process. Accordingly, you can think about the idea one day to understand it, think it over again the next day to analyze it, and consider the *maskana* on the third day.

Once you have completed the process of contemplating an idea or *maamar*, you should continue to think over the same idea again and again day after day until it is fully internalized. This can take a few weeks or even a few months, depending on the person and circumstances.

You can also arrange a system for yourself when to think Chassidus on a basic level (for example, every day before davening) and when to think Chassidus at greater length, following the entire process explained above (for example, during the Shabbos davening).

Thinking Chassidus Before Davening

Additionally, the Frierdiker Rebbe explains[148] that there are two ideas in thinking Chassidus before davening:

1. To reflect upon the idea that Hashem is standing over you and watching you. You should realize that speaking to Hashem, the King of Kings, is a serious thing and should not be taken lightly.

    (This idea ties in with what the Rebbe says many times that one should think over the content of Tanya Chapter 41 every day before davening, where the Alter Rebbe discusses this same concept, that a person is actually standing in front of Hashem.)

2. To think over the Chassidus you have learnt and let the ideas shine in your mind (by understanding them properly).

---

148. See note 139.

The reason why the time before davening is an opportune time to think Chassidus is because it will open your mind and enable it to be receptive to davening. Additionally, the time before davening is a time of *giluy Elokus* when a person is able to grasp and absorb G-dly ideas.[149] In one place, the Rebbe Rashab adds that you can think Chassidus before *Yotzer Or* just like before davening.[150]

❦ Novelty and Consistency

Another important idea is that there are two elements in thinking Chassidus when davening: novelty and consistency.

The first element is to think over the new ideas you have studied that day. Thinking over what you have learnt will ensure a proper understanding of the material (as explained above), which is essential for any *avodah*. Additionally, it helps preserve a feeling of novelty, that you always have something new and interesting on which to contemplate.

This idea is consistent with the answer commonly given by the Rebbe when asked what to think about when davening. The Rebbe would often answer that one should think over what he is currently learning.[151]

The second element is to have a *maamar* or *inyan* you think about each day over a certain period of time, for example, for a few weeks or months. This *maamar* should be one you have already studied, thought about, and properly reviewed. Then, you can take that *maamar*, think it through again, analyze it, and reflect on the practical lesson that can be taken from it.

---

149. See *Kuntres HaTefillah* Chapter 11.
150. See ibid.
151. I have heard from several *chassidishe Yidden* that this was often the Rebbe's response.

A possible method that can be adopted is to think over a new idea before davening and think through the set *maamar* during davening. You can stop at a point during davening relevant to the ideas discussed in the *maamar*, before *Yotzer Or*, or anywhere else. There are no specific rules where to stop and think; each person should find the place in davening that's right for him and think over the *maamar*.

Similarly, there are no rules how long to spend thinking over the same *maamar*. The idea is that the *maamar* should be thought over until it becomes internalized. This certainly can't take less than a week or two, but the exact length depends on the situation, the type of person, the nature of the *maamar*, and so on.

This second element of thinking Chassidus must be done with consistency. The only way for the ideas of a *maamar* to permeate a person's mind and heart is by thinking them over again and again until it becomes his natural way of thinking.

This isn't so exciting, because something real isn't always exciting. A person who owns a car and has a driving license doesn't get excited by driving, because it's part of the reality of life. By contrast, someone who is learning how to drive is excited because it's new for him. The same is true, *lehavdil*, about thinking Chassidus. If the idea is real, it doesn't have to be exciting; it just has to be real. When you first learned about and discovered the idea, it was exciting, but now it's part of your life.[152]

---

152. A perhaps more fitting *mashal* can be given from a *baal teshuvah* who has become *frum*. At first, everything in Yiddishkeit is new and exciting. After some time has passed, although he may retain his passion for his belief and commitment to Torah and mitzvos, he will lose the excitement he once had because it's not new anymore. Instead, he will feel a deep sense of satisfaction that he has found the right path and is living with the truth he had always wanted.

In order to retain the feeling of excitement, you can integrate a new explanation into the *maamar* you think about every day or have a new idea to think about. Additionally, you can think over what you learned in Chassidus that day, as explained above.

There were Chassidim who davened with the same *maamar* for years, and some, for their entire life. The Frierdiker Rebbe mentions[153] that chassidim of old would learn a *maamar* ten or fifteen times, and even then they felt as if they were only on the threshold of the *maamar*. After thinking over the *maamar* twenty to thirty times, they were able to begin appreciating the *Elokus* within the ideas.

The Rebbe Rashab thought over certain *maamarim* of the Rebbe Maharash sixty times. The Rebbe related that he asked the Frierdiker Rebbe about this, and the Frierdiker Rebbe explained that each time someone thinks over a *maamar* he understands it better. It's possible, he continued, that the difference between the sixtieth time and the fifty-ninth time will be as drastic as the difference between the fifty-ninth time and the first time![154]

༄ Explaining Chassidus to Yourself as You Would to Another

When thinking over a *maamar*, you should explain it to yourself in the same manner as you would explain it to someone else.

Similarly, a person who works hard to develop an awareness and feeling for Hashem in davening will have great excitement (התפעלות) at first. Over time, however, this is replaced with a deep feeling of satisfaction from being a Yid who is connected to Hashem (מ'איז צופרידען אז מ'איז א איד וואס פארבינדט זיך מיטן אויבערשטן).

153. See note 139.
154. *Sichah* of *Shabbos Parshas Shemini*, 5710 (*Toras Menachem* 5710, p. 29).

Imagine you are giving a *shiur* in the *maamar*. You go through the *maamar* piece by piece, focusing on each part and explaining it well so that the richness of the *maamar* will be brought out. Now imagine you are *farbrenging* about the *maamar*. You bring out the lesson that can be taken from the *maamar* and explain how it can affect one's perspective and be applied to one's daily conduct.

Back to real life, this is exactly what you should do when thinking over a *maamar*. You must teach it to yourself, *farbreng* about it with yourself, and inspire yourself.

When explaining a *maamar* to another, you would first make sure he understands the basic idea. You can then offer more depth about the idea, and after that you can bring out the lesson. This is also how you should explain the *maamar* to yourself. First you should think through the *maamar* exactly as it is written, similar to the way a *maamar* is reviewed by heart. (The difference is that here you are reviewing the *maamar* in thought.) After going through a *maamar* in this manner a few times, you can think it over and analyze the new ideas that can be gained from the *maamar*. You can then focus on deducing the lesson that can be taken from the *maamar*.[155]

Another point:

When explaining a *maamar* to someone else, it's sometimes possible to go straight from the basic idea to the lesson that can be derived from it, without adding to what the *maamar* says. Similarly, when explaining a *maamar* to yourself, what's of primary importance is to understand the *maamar* itself (or the *perek Tanya* and so on) and its lesson. The second step of analyzing and examining the *maamar* isn't always

---

155. See the letter of R. Nisan Nemenov quoted in the introduction to *Chassidus Mivu'eres, Avodas HaTefillah*.

necessary, as long as the ideas of the *maamar* are understood properly and the lesson is applied.

As mentioned above, when describing the *mashal* from learning Gemara, the Frierdiker Rebbe explains that to be able to analyze a *sugya* and recognize the novelty of each point requires a sharp mind and cannot be done by every individual. Similarly, examining the depth of the *maamar* to appreciate its richness depends on the person, the *maamar*, and so on.

Making a System That Works

As can be seen from the above, there are different ways how the three steps and two elements discussed in this chapter can be split up. As mentioned before, there are no specific rules that are set in stone; each person should figure out a system that works for him, with the help and guidance of a *mashpia* or *chaver*. The main thing is to go through the three steps of understanding, analyzing (if applicable), and applying the *maamar*, and to have two "tracks" in thinking Chassidus—one consisting of new ideas, and the second, of the same *inyan* being worked on slowly but surely until it permeates and changes you and your perspective.

Similarly, although it's important to figure out the lesson of the *maamar*, this doesn't mean that whenever you think Chassidus you have to think of the lesson. Based on the system you have set up for yourself, there will be times when you will focus on understanding the ideas of the *maamar*, and there will be times when you will focus on the lesson of the *maamar* and its practical application.

Thinking Chassidus isn't meant to be a complicated, detailed process; it should be a natural part of your life. It should become part of your system that you think through what you learn in Chassidus until, over time, it is truly internalized.

This can be compared to a relationship between two people. The first time they meet, they get to know each other very vaguely. The next time they spend time together, they connect to each other a little bit more. Over time, they get to know each other better and better until a genuine feeling of friendship and affection is developed. It's a process that doesn't happen overnight and can only be reached one step at a time.

Similarly, when a person starts learning Chassidus, the concepts may appear abstract and even a bit strange. Slowly but surely, he becomes familiar with the concepts until he begins to appreciate what they really mean and the messages they impart. Then, when he davens, he builds up a connection with the life-changing depth of these teachings until he develops a strong feeling for Hashem.

This process can only happen with a lot of effort, but that's how any good relationship is formed. The main thing is to view having a *pnimiyus'dike* connection to Hashem as an integral part of your life,[156] and you can then figure out for yourself the exact details of how to make the process flow smoothly.

---

156. See the end of the *maamar* "Rava Chazya LeRav Hamnuna" (*Sefer Hamaamorim Kuntreisim*, Vol. 1, pp. 231–232) where the Frierdiker Rebbe uses a number of strong expressions to illustrate how personal this is.

Chapter 7.
REAL *HISBONENUS*

Real *hisbonenus* that will bring about a complete change in a person is much more than just reviewing a *maamar* in thought a few times. To truly connect to an idea in *Elokus*, it is necessary to do the following:

1. You should study the subject discussed in the *maamar* thoroughly. If the subject is not fully explained in this particular *maamar*, you should join together information from various *maamarim* until the entire concept is complete in your mind.[157] In other words, you should *learn* and *understand* the concept thoroughly.

2. You should organize all the explanations you have studied on the topic into one clear picture in your mind. You should put together all the different ideas and see how they complement each other and provide a better understanding of the topic as a whole. In other words, you should *grasp* the concept properly with all its details.

3. You should think over the entire idea until you understand it well enough to explain to someone else, even if he is on a much lower level than you (for example, to a person on *mivtzoyim*). You should explain the concept to yourself until you are logically convinced that it is true. In other words, you should internalize

---

157. Of course, although this is the most ideal way, you can think over a concept of Chassidus even after having learnt only one *maamar*.

the concept until it is *true in actuality* and isn't just an abstract idea in the books.

4. You should think over this idea every day until you feel that it has become part of your physical reality. In other words, you should internalize the concept until it is *true in your personal life* and not just true in general.

We will give a practical example from a *hisbonenus* on the topic of *hashgachah pratis*.

1. The first step is to learn the various *sichos* and *maamarim* that explain the concept of *hashgachah pratis* with all of its aspects. By way of example, ideas that would be explored would include the following:

    a. Awareness of *hashgachah pratis* will result in the realization that there is nothing to worry about since everything is preordained by Hashem.

    b. *Hashgachah pratis* is related to the idea that Hashem is constantly creating everything and that each detail has a purpose.

    Similarly, any other aspect that can be seen as part of this topic should be researched.

2. The second step is to put together the various explanations of this concept and organize them in your mind until you see how they work together.

3. After researching the topic thoroughly, you should think it over one section at a time until you can see the entire picture how Hashem truly has everything planned out to the smallest detail and how each and every detail is important and necessary in fulfilling the purpose of creation.

4. After thinking it over and actually seeing this picture, you should explain to yourself how this is true in your personal life as well, that every detail of your life is planned out by Hashem Himself and is of the utmost importance to Him.

This process is very different from merely thinking over a *maamar*. It is an extremely long process, but it is the "longer shorter way"; ultimately, this is the only way to reach the desired goal. However, to be ready to undertake such a journey, you must first get used to thinking Chassidus in general, because even thinking Chassidus on a basic level can be difficult. You should first grow accustomed to thinking over *maamarim*, Tanya, and so on every day for at least a few months, and when it isn't (as) difficult for you to think Chassidus for five to ten minutes without interruption, you can begin the process of real *hisbonenus* with the help of a *mashpia*.

A *mashpia*[158] once advised a student to think over a certain idea in Chassidus at length. The student said that he would rather think over the words of the *maamar (osiyos harav)* instead of thinking over the idea itself.

Some time later, the student had *yechidus* with the Rebbe, and he mentioned what his *mashpia* had told him and what he had answered. The Rebbe told him that during the week, when he doesn't have as much time available to think Chassidus, he can suffice with thinking the words of the *maamar*. On Shabbos, however, he should follow his *mashpia's* advice and think over the idea itself at length.

We can see from this that there is a definite advantage to thinking over the idea itself as explained above, but since this is a long and involved process, it's possible that one will only have the time and effort available for this on Shabbos. How-

---

158. R. Yitzchok Meir Gurary.

ever, one must keep in mind that this is the only way to achieve a full grasp of and connection to the ideas of Chassidus.

The third volume of this series will explore, with Hashem's help, a number of topics and ideas that a person can use for this purpose.

Chapter 8.
PUTTING EFFORT INTO THINKING CHASSIDUS

🕮 IT'S ALL ABOUT THE DETAILS

The Rebbe Rashab explains at length in *Kuntres HaTefillah* and *Kuntres HaAvodah* that the only way *hisbonenus* can affect a person is if it is done in a detailed manner, as opposed to a general overview. This means that you can't suffice with just summarizing the *maamar* and thinking over the summary for thirty seconds or a minute; you must think through the *maamar* with all its details in order to experience what the *maamar* is saying.

(Although there is no exact amount of time for which one must think Chassidus, as a general rule, experience has shown that to do this correctly takes at least five minutes.)

This is different than the concept of thinking the *chassidishe pirush hamilos*. For that purpose, it's enough to think over the main idea of the *maamar* that explains that part of davening. However, that isn't meant to replace the idea of thinking Chassidus, which refers specifically to a genuine, detailed contemplation. What it's supposed to be is a *supplement* to thinking Chassidus: in addition to thinking through a *maamar* properly (and thinking the simple *pirush hamilos* of davening), you should try to think about the deeper meaning of the words.

It's true that when thinking through a *maamar*, it's helpful to summarize the ideas after thinking them through in detail, and the summary can then provide even more clarity than was gained by thinking through the details alone. However, thinking over a summary by itself isn't considered a proper contemplation.

The reason for this is because an entity can only be grasped by its edges. When a person wants to grasp a physical object, he must first locate its parameters, and these parameters must be small enough for him to wrap his hand around them. Similarly, in order to grasp an idea, one must find its parameters, its definition and limits, and each idea must be small enough for the mind to process. The details are the "handle" with which one is able to grasp the concept; by grasping each detail one at a time (each detail being small enough to process), you will be able to grasp the entire concept properly. Merely thinking over a summary, by contrast, will not enable you to grasp the idea properly.

(Evidence to this is the fact that when you suffice with a summary, you typically cannot explain the idea using different words. If you would have truly grasped the idea, you would be able to explain it without using the same words as the *maamar*.)

❦ Effort Brings Success

Thinking through an idea with all its details is much harder than thinking over a short summary of the concept, but this is the way you will be able to connect to it. In Tanya (Chapter 42) the Alter Rebbe explains that to achieve *daas* in *Elokus*, you can't suffice with studying *sefarim* and listening to the explanations of *tamidei chachamim*; you must work hard to connect your mind to the idea until it is as real to you as a physical object. This requires a lot of effort, because you have to think through the ideas clearly, explain them to yourself, and bring out the lessons that can be applied from them. But *Chazal* have promised us, *"yagata u'matzasa taamin,"* "If you have worked hard and succeeded, you can be believed."

Contemplating an idea from Chassidus is something you must toil at. Don't view spending a long time thinking over a *maamar* as something burdensome. You shouldn't satisfy yourself with thinking Chassidus for a couple of minutes and then say, "I was *yoitzei* my obligation to think Chassidus." You should think through the *maamar* and *farbreng* with yourself until you feel that it means something to you and that you have really connected to the idea.

On some days, when you're in a rush, you can think Chassidus for five minutes and that will be enough, but your general attitude must be that this is something into which you invest time and effort. Everyone knows that in order to become a *baki* in Torah, a person must put effort into learning. Can you imagine transforming your natural tendencies and elevating yourself without effort? Doing that surely requires even more effort! Explain to yourself that this is a worthwhile investment and that every ounce of effort devoted to this end will be well spent.

Some Practical Tips

When a person starts to think Chassidus, he may find it difficult to concentrate and can suddenly discover that he is "spacing out" and thinking about other things when he is supposed to be thinking about the *maamar*. If this happens to you, don't be deterred. It's only natural to be easily distracted if you are not used to concentrating for a long time on a single idea. After a few months of thinking Chassidus, it will start getting easier to concentrate, and eventually you will be able to think through an entire *maamar* from beginning to end without spacing out in the middle. So if you find yourself spacing out when thinking Chassidus, don't worry about it too much; just return to what you were thinking about as if nothing happened, and after working on this for a while you will overcome this problem.

As mentioned before, there are no exact rules as to where in davening you should stop and think Chassidus. You should find the place that works best for you, whether before *Hodu*, before *Ashrei*, or anywhere else.

When you reach the spot where you will be thinking Chassidus, you should stop saying the words of davening and think instead. You shouldn't think Chassidus while saying the words; at that time you should be thinking the *pirush hamilos*, not Chassidus.

If the chazzan reaches kaddish or the like when you're in the middle of thinking, just stop where you are, answer, and then go back to the idea you were thinking about. Just as there are stopping points when reading a book (for example, the end of a paragraph), there are "stopping points" in the idea you are thinking about, so you can stop and answer and then go back to the most recent "stopping point."

The main thing is to make thinking Chassidus into a habit. Just like you must learn Chassidus every day and say the words of davening every day and after a while it becomes routine, you should think Chassidus every day until it becomes a daily routine. Make sure that not a day goes by without thinking about Hashem.

 Davening on Shabbos

There is a big difference between the weekday and Shabbos davening. The Alter Rebbe mentions in Tanya[159] that on Shabbos even working people can and must daven properly, meaning that they must think and become inspired by Chassidus. Similarly, *bochurim* in yeshiva and *yungeleit* in *kollel* have a greater opportunity to daven on Shabbos than they have during the week, because during the week they are limited to the *sedarim* of the yeshiva or *kollel*, but on Shabbos they can daven without looking at the clock. Furthermore, Shabbos is a special time, an *eis ratzon*, when it is much easier to daven and attain a real understanding of and feeling for Chassidus. One can accomplish a lot more on Shabbos than we think is usually possible.

Accordingly, on Shabbos you should make sure to learn (or finish off or review) an entire *maamar* and think it over completely. You should make this be your priority, that on Shabbos you will think Chassidus no matter how long it will take, and you will try to truly understand and connect to what you have learnt and gain inspiration from it. This will give you the inspiration and motivation to learn Chassidus and daven throughout the week.[160] The only thing that's needed is to realize how important it is until it becomes your priority.

---

159. אגרת הקדש ס"א.

160. See *Torah Or, Parshas Noach, Maamar Mayim Rabim*, where the Alter Rebbe explains that all of a person's davening during the week is an extension of his davening on Shabbos.

Chapter 9.
ENJOYING CHASSIDUS

As important it is to put effort into davening, it is of at least equal importance not to look at davening as an obligation but as something *enjoyable*. The only reason we must sometimes force ourselves to daven is because, as is true with anything in life, if we really want something to happen, we must sometimes force ourselves to make it happen. Our emotions are designed in such a way that we don't always feel like doing what's best for us; as a result, we must sometimes force ourselves to do things even though we don't feel like doing them. In reality, however, davening is something extremely enjoyable.

In *Kuntres Umaayon*[161] the Rebbe Rashab describes various levels of pleasure. He explains that for a person, the highest level of pleasure lies in intellect. In intellect itself, the ultimate pleasure can be found in the G-dly intellect of Torah, and in Torah itself, in *pnimiyus hatorah*. By learning *pnimiyus hatorah* you can come to recognize and feel *ruchniyus*. Your *neshamah* leaves behind a state of being coarse and concerned with physicality, and instead connects with a state of becoming refined and spiritual.

In *Kuntres HaAvodah*[162] the Rebbe Rashab explains that if a person thinks Chassidus as if it were a chore, it is unlikely that he will develop true feelings (of love and fear of

---

161. בתחילתו.
162. ע' מב.

Hashem). Thinking Chassidus will only bring about such feelings if you are excited about Chassidus and enjoy thinking about and connecting to it.

A businessman doesn't need to force himself to think about his business and figure out how to improve it; it comes to him naturally because this is where his excitement lies. Similarly, it should be natural for someone who appreciates a little of the infinite depth of Chassidus to be excited to think about and live with these incredibly beautiful realities.

How can a person arouse an enjoyment in thinking Chassidus?

One piece of advice is to realize the uniqueness of the subject matter you are thinking about. As the Rebbe Rashab explains there,[163] before one thinks Chassidus he should recognize that he isn't thinking about an ordinary idea that can be conceived by the human mind; he is contemplating on an idea of *Elokus*, which is infinitely higher than anything that exists in this material world. You are trying to connect your mind and elevate yourself to a reality that is entirely beyond your present state.

Another way you can heighten your enjoyment is through *nigunim*. The Alter Rebbe explains that *neginah* can help a person break free from his limitations and draws forth from the essence of one's *neshamah*.[164] The Frierdiker Rebbe explains that *nigunim* open up a passageway between *chaya yechida* and *nara"n*, the essence of the *neshamah* and the *neshamah* as it is enclothed within the body. *Osiyos hanegina*, he explains—the letters of song—are *osiyos atzmiyim*, letters that express the essence; or as the Alter Rebbe puts it, song is the language of the soul.

---

163. קונטרס העבודה שם.
164. ראה ד"ה יבל הוא הי' (בתו"א פ' בראשית) ע' ז, ג.

This means that a *nigun* can help you understand and feel the truth of the *neshamah* and of *Elokus*, and it can enable you to "get outside of your box" and think in a more spiritual and profound way. The Frierdiker Rebbe expressed this idea when he said in the name of the Rebbe Maharash that if a person is afflicted with *timtum hamoach* (i.e., he is unable to understand Chassidus properly), thinking Chassidus deeply may not suffice. Sometimes, it is only with the help of a *nigun* that his mind will be able to open up to Chassidus.[165]

This is why chassidim sing during davening, sometimes before davening, sometimes in the middle of davening, and sometimes after davening. In addition, in Lubavitch there is a *seder nigunim*, a *seder* dedicated to simply singing *nigunim*, as this itself can help a person attain proper feelings during davening. Even if you just teach yourself new *nigunim* or listen to them before going to sleep or at some other time, they will eventually infiltrate your mind and you will be able to find the right *nigun* to express yourself during davening.

---

165. סה"ש תש"ג ע' 115–113.

Section 4:
CHESHBON HANEFESH

INTRODUCTION

Although seemingly an unrelated concept, the idea of making a *cheshbon hanefesh* is an integral part of davening, for two reasons.

First of all, the main goal of davening is to be inspired to fulfill Hashem's will through keeping the Torah and mitzvos properly, which is accomplished by developing a love and fear of Hashem. The Zohar compares love and fear to the wings of a bird. Just as wings enable a bird to fly, so do love and fear of Hashem elevate our Torah and mitzvos and enhance their affect on us and the world. Since real davening means to know Hashem and develop a love and fear of Him, it thus follows that an important part of davening is to ensure that we fulfill His will properly.

It is therefore important to translate every inspiration you have into something practical, and to be constantly aware of exactly where you are holding and what you must still accomplish in your *avodas Hashem*. For this to happen, you must frequently make a *cheshbon hanefesh*.

A *cheshbon hanefesh* is also known as a *cheshbon tzedek*, an honest account, since it isn't always easy to overcome our self-love and honestly come to terms with the fact that we have made a mistake and need to change. This is why it's important to make this a regular habit, so we can overcome our ego bit by bit through commitment and *kabalas ol* to serve Hashem even if it requires change.

A second reason why making a *cheshbon hanefesh* is necessary for davening is because achieving an awareness of Hashem means you are searching for Him and trying to find Him in your personal life. In order to truly recognize that you need to find Hashem in your life, you must realize that your true identity is your *neshamah,* and you must know what you can be and where you are presently—all parts of the *cheshbon hanefesh* process, as explained in this section.

Chapter 1.
KNOWING WHO WE ARE AND WHERE WE ARE GOING

Chassidus and Kabbalah view *Krias Shema Al Hamitah* as a special time for making a *cheshbon hanefesh*, an accounting of your spiritual standing.

To be able to make a proper *cheshbon hanefesh*, you must first set up a personal *seder*, a program of spiritual growth, through which you conduct your day. This *seder* should encompass every aspect of *avodas Hashem*, such as learning Torah, davening, acting with *ahavas yisroel*, doing everything *lesheim shamayim*, and so on.

However, before embarking on this spiritual journey, a person must be aware of three underlying principles.

The first principle is the idea of *bechirah chafshis*, free will.

The Alter Rebbe explains in Tanya (Chap. 14) that every person has the ability to be a *beinoni* at any given moment. Whenever a person is overcome with a desire to indulge in a *taavah*, whether permissible or, *chas veshalom*, forbidden, he can always stay in control by telling himself: "I don't want to be separated from Hashem for even a single moment. What I truly desire is to connect to Hashem through His Torah and mitzvos, since a hidden, intrinsic love for Hashem is found within my heart. How can I go against His will if this will weaken my connection with Hashem?!" Thoughts such as these can help him overcome his desire and even lead him to perform a mitzvah instead.

Later in Tanya (Chap. 17), the Alter Rebbe explains how aiming to fulfill all of the Torah and mitzvos is a very accessible goal. Everyone has a brain and can think about any idea he so desires. Thus, if a person will focus his mind on his love for Hashem, he will automatically be able to control himself, since the nature of the mind is to control the heart.

We can derive two things from this. First, we learn the basic idea that our intellect controls our emotions. We have the power to overcome our negative desires and act based on our inner conviction to do what's right. Second, if we would recognize that we possess a hidden love for Hashem and an inherent desire to serve Him and not be separated from Him, it would give us the power and motivating strength to serve Hashem even when it's difficult.

Thus, the first principle is to recognize that we have *bechirah chafshis* to choose what we want to do, and together with that we have *moach shalit al haleiv*—the ability for the mind to control the heart, a critical element in the nature of a person. Every human being has the ability to choose how to lead his life and how to respond to any situation he is placed in. We aren't forced to conduct ourselves in a certain way, not by our environment, our family background, or even our past deeds. At every moment, we are given the chance to realize what we should be doing and act according to our value system, based on our recognition that Hashem is our King and that we do what He desires, and not as dictated by the world around us, our environment, or our past. We can think and realize what we are here for and act based on our conviction to fulfill our mission and purpose.[166]

---

166. See *Rambam, Hilchos Teshuvah,* Chapter 5, where he explains that free choice is one of the foundations of Torah and mitzvos, and that the only way someone can do *teshuvah* is if he realizes he has free will.

The second principle is that we have to know who we are and what we really care about. In other words, there are two questions we have to ask ourselves: Who am I, and what am I here for.

Who am I—a Yid, a *cheilek eloka mima'al mamash*. My *neshamah* is invested within a *nefesh hasichlis*, a *nefesh habahamis*, and a body, in order that they too may be connected to Hashem. In truth, I really love Hashem and don't want to be separated from Him at any cost, and the only thing I really care about is Hashem.

What am I here for? To serve Hashem. To make a *dirah bitachtonim*, a dwelling place for Hashem in this world, by learning Torah, doing mitzvos, davening, and performing all of my physical actions *lesheim shamayim*. When a person will truly understand this, he will come to the realization that every aspect of his life is part of this mission. Hence, anything that does not directly benefit this goal—and especially if it clearly opposes it—has no place in his life. With this focus, he can then choose to subordinate any feelings or distractions and act based on his desire to follow this mission, no matter what's going on around him.

Chapter 2.
MAKING A *SEDER*

Once we know who we are and what we are here for, the third principle comes into place: to figure out how to achieve all this in actuality. (This doesn't mean to say that planning how to serve Hashem in practicality must wait until you have fully appreciated and are totally dedicated to Him. Rather, the intention here is that you must realize that all this is true if you want your *hachlatos* and plan to succeed. Furthermore, if you want them to continue to succeed, it is important to constantly remind yourself that this is what you really care about and that you can really achieve it.)

To accomplish this, it is very helpful (if not essential) to create an actual *seder* of how you will implement this recognition. Write down your plans on paper and categorize them according to the different categories in your *avodas Hashem*.

For example, standard categories would consist of (but are not be limited to) Torah, *tefillah, ahavas yisroel, hiskrashus, kiyum mitzvos behiddur,* and doing everything *lesheim shamayim.* In each section, specify in detail what it includes and what Hashem wants from you. Torah, for instance, is comprised of Chassidus and *nigleh,* with each one encompassing many areas. In *tefillah,* as well, there are many components, such as understanding the *pirush hamilos* and thinking Chassidus. When setting up a program for spiritual growth, you must organize each area with all its details to ensure that you know what you must accomplish and where you are headed.

Without question, it is vital to have a *mashpia* with whom you can consult regarding these issues, as a guide to establishing an appropriate *seder*. However, your *mashpia* cannot create your *seder* for you. It is up to you to organize all the details, as otherwise it is impossible to be completely aware of everything you need to do and to figure out how to wisely use your time.

Once you've taken the time to consider exactly what Hashem wants from you, you should arrange a schedule that will incorporate all of these things without leaving out anything important. With the help of your *mashpia* as well as close friends, you will be able to decide what should be implemented right away and what should be set aside for a later stage.

Once a person has reached this point—he realizes that his mind can control his heart, he knows his goal in life, and he creates a *seder* in *avodas Hashem*—he can then keep track of his achievements and plan ahead to decide what should be worked on next. This is what should be done at *Krias Shema Al Hamitah* every night. This is the time to reflect on these two things: if you are keeping to your *seder* and what you need to continue doing.

To this end, in addition to writing down a general *seder* in *avodas Hashem*, you should keep a daily (or weekly) planner where you can schedule when you will do each thing and arrange that you have enough time for all of them.

❧ Long Term and Short Term Goals

When making a *seder*, it is helpful to know that there are

two types of goals: those that are long term and those that are short term.

Long term goals take an extended period of time and require much effort to accomplish. For example, learning the entire Talmud Bavli can take seven and a half years when keeping to a one-*daf*-per-day ratio. This can sometimes take more than an hour a day (if one learns it slowly and properly). In the same vein, to learn the entire *Hemshech Ayin Beis* can take three to four years if you spend the proper amount of time studying it. Going through the entire davening with *kavanah* can take years to accomplish as well. For these goals, you need to plan in advance how much time you will need to spend each day, week, and so on in order to achieve them.

Short term goals are ones that only take a few weeks or months, and you can see the end result from where you are now. Examples of such resolutions are basic proper davening, learning *chitas* and Rambam, and so on. These are more urgent tasks that must be worked on first.

The reason we need to differentiate between these two types of goals is so that we will have the foresight how to place them in our schedule. We need to consider those goals that must be accomplished immediately, together with those we want to accomplish over a lengthier course of time. This will ensure that we will strategically plan out how to accomplish all the things that are truly important to us. When you have written your *seder* in *avodas Hashem* and have included both your long term and short term goals, it's much easier to figure out how to put them in your schedule and make sure that nothing is left out.

Chapter 3.
MAKING A *CHESHBON HANEFESH*

Once you have a *seder,* you can see by *Krias Shema Al Hamitah* if you are keeping up to it. This is the time to think about the past day and consider if you kept up to your *seder* and acted properly.¹⁶⁷

In addition to the daily *cheshbon hanefesh,* there is also a *cheshbon hanefesh* we conduct on Erev Shabbos or Erev Rosh Chodesh, when we think about the entire previous week or month. Special occasions, like the month of Elul, a personal birthday, Yud Shevat, Gimmel Tammuz, and similar dates are a time to look a little bit deeper into ourselves, to consider whether we are really the way Hashem and the Rebbe want us to be.¹⁶⁸

---

167. I heard from Rabbi Moshe Feller that he once asked the Rebbe what to do if he is too tired to say *Krias Shema Al Hamitah* with a *cheshbon hanefesh* before going to sleep. The Rebbe answered that in such a situation, he should do so right after *Maariv*.

Alternatively, if you did not manage to make a *cheshbon hanefesh* before going to sleep, you should at least do so the next morning as a preparation for davening. The Alter Rebbe explains (in the second letter printed at the end of *Siddur Tehillas Hashem*) that before davening a person should make a *cheshbon hanefesh* accompanied by *teshuvah,* and he should then remove any trace of sadness from his heart by focusing on the joy of seeing the glory of Hashem as it is accessible to us during davening. This is not the usual *seder* for our generation, since it's difficult for us to change our feelings from one extreme to the other in succession, but it could work from time to time (for example, when one wasn't able make a *cheshbon hanefesh* at night).

168. ראה תורת מנחם ח"א ע' 175. היום יום י"א ניסן.

Once you become accustomed to having a routine *cheshbon hanefesh* for your external actions, you can incorporate a deeper kind of contemplation. This *pniyimus'dike cheshbon hanefesh* is to see if you have the proper feelings for what you are doing, for example, to see if you have genuine *ahavas yisroel*, appropriate concentration when davening, proper intentions when eating and sleeping, and so on.

You don't need to examine all of your feelings every day. Rather, the idea is that you should be aware of yourself and your standing in *avodas Hashem*. You need to consider not only your actions but also the attitude behind them, and resolve how to advance in the proper direction with your actions as well as with your feelings and outlook.

We are only expected to think about this for a few minutes every day, but if we do this continuously we will notice steady changes in our lives.

The Frierdiker Rebbe related[169] that a certain chossid of the Rebbe Maharash was once told by the Rebbe to fast for six hundred days. The chossid couldn't understand how such an undertaking is possible. The Rebbe Maharash explained that he didn't mean it to be taken literally. Not eating isn't called fasting; it's called dieting! Rather, he intended that this person should spend fifteen minutes every day thinking about his spiritual level for a total of six hundred days. The chossid followed the Rebbe's instructions. When he returned afterward to the Rebbe, not only had his external actions changed for the better, but his entire personality and essence were transformed.

The Frierdiker Rebbe concluded that we can learn from this how important it is to designate time daily to think about ourselves. Whether you spend fifteen minutes a day or just a

---

169. *Lekutei Diburim*, Vol. 4, p. 136 (English); pp. 1211–1212 (Hebrew).

few minutes (if fifteen is too difficult), it's very important to think about improving yourself on a daily basis, until you will see significant changes, with Hashem's help.

Chapter 4.
MAKING *HACHLATOS*

When a person makes a *cheshbon hanefesh* and sees that there is an area that requires improvement, he makes a *hachlatah*, a firm resolution to either add in the positive or refrain from the negative.

It may be helpful to keep the following points in mind when deciding on a *hachlatah*:

1. Choose something that is high on your priority list. For example, if someone isn't learning *chitas* or Rambam and he is also not davening with a minyan, he should begin by resolving to daven with a minyan. (See above, Chapter 2, "Making a *Seder*," that you should create your personal *seder* in serving Hashem with specific priorities of what will be worked on immediately and what will be set aside for a later time.)

2. Decide on something you know you can *realistically* accomplish, considering your current situation. For example, someone who is too busy to learn Rambam or has difficulty grasping it should first make a *hachlatah* to learn one *perek* a day (or *Sefer Hamitzvos*). Once he has kept his *hachlatah* for a few months, he can consider starting to learn three *perakim* a day. If he were to immediately begin by learning three *perakim* a day, even if he manages to accomplish this for a short period of time, he will "crash" soon after and won't be able to continue. (This is merely an example to bring

out the idea, although for some it might be feasible to "jump" into learning three *perakim* right away.)

3. Resolve to follow your *hachlatah* for a *short and specific amount of time*. For example, if you resolve to start waking up early, or to learn a specific amount of material every day, try it out for one or two weeks, and during that time push yourself to keep the *hachlatah*. If it works well, you can extend it for another few weeks. Generally, you should never make a *hachlatah* to do something forever. With the end of your goal in sight, you can tell yourself, "It's only for a short period of time. I can definitely do it."

4. Commit yourself to *one hachlatah* at a time. If you challenge yourself with many *hachlatos*, then you will lose the willpower and concentration necessary to keep them all. Only if you accept one *hachlatah* at a time and concentrate your efforts on it can you hope for it to succeed. (You may decide to choose one *hachlatah* that you will keep no matter what, and another one that you will fulfill when you are able to, but there can only be one *main hachlatah* that you will keep regardless of the circumstances.)[170]

---

170. See *Sefer Hasichos* 5703, pp. 228–229, where the Frierdiker Rebbe says (quoting the Rebbe Rashab) that if you want to help another person rectify his misdoings, you should only advise him to change one thing at a time. This is for two reasons: (1) You can't restrict all of his desires; you can only limit some of them while allowing others. (2) Through advising him to change one step at a time, he will realize that you truly care about him and aren't simply trying to undermine his desires and offend him.

Obviously, the first reason also applies to a person working on improving his own character.

For more on how to change and make *hachlatos* and a *cheshbon hanefesh*, it is recommended to learn *Klalei Hachinuch Veha'hadrachah* from the Frierdiker Rebbe (printed at the end of *Sefer Hasichos* 5703, and also translated into English as *The Principles of Education and Guidance*).

5. Daven to Hashem to help you persevere with your decision. During davening (in *Shema Koleinu*,[171] before the second *Yihiyu Leratzon*,[172] or by *Krias Shema Al Hamitah*), ask Hashem to give you the strength to continue and not be held back by anything, especially by your past habits. Also, when you write to the Rebbe,[173] ask the Rebbe to daven to Hashem on your behalf.

6. Tell a friend about your *hachlatah*. The Rebbe said that at birthday *farbrengens* one should make a public *hachlatah*, since such a *hachlatah* has more potential to succeed. Similarly, any *hachlatah* disclosed to a close friend is more likely to succeed because he will encourage you to keep it. (See below, Chapter 5, "Writing a *Duch*," for more on this subject.)

R. Yitzchak Meir Gurary once came to the Rebbe with a dilemma probably familiar to many. He would become inspired by *farbrengens* and accept positive *hachlatos*, but his enthusiasm wouldn't last and he wouldn't end up keeping his *hachlatos*. The Rebbe explained that the general reason a *hachlatah* doesn't last is either because the inspiration isn't immediately expressed with something tangible, or because the *hachlatah* was simply too big to stick to. One has to make sure both that his inspiration is immediately channeled into a concrete decision, and that his decision is small and manageable—מעט מעט אגרשנו.[174]

---

171. See Section 1, Chapter 1.
172. See ibid.
173. See Chapter 5, "Writing a *Duch*."
174. *Derher Magazine*, Iyar 5775, p. 64.

Chapter 5.
WRITING A *DUCH*

In addition to the *cheshbon hanefesh* you should conduct as part of your routine, it is very helpful to write a *din v'cheshbon* to the Rebbe on a regular basis. The reason for this is because a person needs to feel a sense of responsibility to enable him to accomplish as much as he can. If a person's accomplishments are based on what he himself feels is acceptable, they will always be limited. However, when a person writes to the Rebbe, realizing that the Rebbe wants to hear a good report, he will fulfill much more, since he realizes that the Rebbe won't be satisfied with the bare minimum or with mediocre accomplishments. Since he wants to give the Rebbe *nachas,* he will push himself to achieve his utmost.

This also relates to the idea of *knei lecha chaver*—acquire for yourself a friend, meaning that you must work hard to find a true friend. A true friend is someone with whom you can discuss your standing in *avodas Hashem* and gain insight and motivation on how to improve. Also, it is very important to have someone who can help evaluate where you are holding and monitor your improvements, or simply give you reminders to work on those areas you know need improvement but have a hard time actually implementing.

Needless to say, this is also the idea of having a *mashpia,* someone who is on a higher level who can help guide you and elevate you. There is a common factor between writing to the Rebbe, speaking with friends, and consulting with a *mashpia:* since a person loves himself and has a natural tendency to overlook his shortcomings, he can't evaluate his situation with complete accuracy and objectivity. Only by "leaving" himself and presenting his situation to an outside person can he reach an honest evaluation and achieve true improvement.

Chapter 6.
TESHUVAH

———⋙∞⋘———

Teshuvah is an important part of *Krias Shema Al Hamitah* (and vice versa—*Krias Shema Al Hamitah* is an important part of *teshuvah*).

As explained above, *Krias Shema Al Hamitah* is a time to think about your conduct throughout the day and acknowledge that you need to improve. When making this calculation, there are two ideas to consider: (1) Which areas have I worked on but still need improvement? (2) In which aspects did I go wrong?

The first idea, as explained above at length, requires having a *seder* so you can monitor and improve your positive conduct. You should evaluate your actions, consider if or why you aren't keeping up to your *seder*, and resolve to correct your behavior. The second element of "What did I do wrong" is the idea of *teshuvah*.

If you know you have done something wrong, you must at the very least fulfill the most basic element of *teshuvah*. This consists of two parts. Firstly, you must honestly regret your misbehavior, that is, you must think and realize that you should not have done this act and should never do it again. Secondly, you must resolve never to repeat the misdeed again, and you must do whatever necessary to ensure the fulfillment of that decision. You must try to determine what caused it to happen and what you can do to make sure it doesn't repeat itself.

In addition to these two primary components of *teshuvah*, there are two additional aspects that are important as well: (1) To verbally confess your wrongdoing to Hashem, and to verbally express that you regret what you did and will try your utmost not to stumble again. (2) To ask Hashem for forgiveness.[175]

What happens if you did all the above and then messed up again (as happens to most of us most of the time)?

In such a case, you should simply repeat the process, as if you were doing it for the first time. As explained in Tanya,[176] it is difficult for a human being to repeatedly forgive another person for the same offense he committed over and over again. However, since Hashem and his attributes are infinite, He forgives us the thousandth time with the same compassion as the first time, as long as the person continues to do genuine *teshuvah*. Hashem knows we have a *yetzer hara*, that we struggle to overcome it, and that sometimes we don't win the battle. But that doesn't mean we intend to keep repeating our mistakes. We continue to fight, and Hashem accepts that as long as we try to do *teshuvah* as best as we can.

❧ Faith and Joy in *Teshuvah*

An integral idea in *teshuvah* is that you must never give up, and you must have complete faith that Hashem will help you do *teshuvah* and you will definitely succeed. Once you do *teshuvah* as the Torah prescribes, you should continue keeping your *seder* and not feel bad about what happened. On the contrary, you should be joyful that Hashem believes in you and trusts you to overcome your challenges and continue to

---

175. ראה אגה"ת פ"א.
176. ראה אגה"ת שם.

go forward, and you should be happy with the belief that Hashem will surely help you succeed.

The Rebbe explains in a *maamar*[177] that nowadays, the primary way of doing *teshuvah* is with joy. The idea of *tracht gut vet zayn gut* doesn't only apply to physical challenges; it equally applies—and even more so—to spiritual matters. The way we should do *teshuvah* is by thinking positively and trusting that Hashem will help us grow and overcome our challenges.

Thus, even though *teshuvah* is something that must be done, and without it you won't be able to *daven* and serve Hashem properly, it should not lower your spirits. On the contrary, it should bring you tremendous joy and inspire you with the motivation never to give up, because you realize that Hashem is always ready to give you another chance.

---

177. ד"ה מרגלא בפומי' דרבא תשמ"ו.

Chapter 7.
THE PROPER APPROACH TO MAKING A *CHESHBON TZEDEK*

In a *sichah* of *Shabbos Parshas Noach*, 5752,[178] the Rebbe explains how one should approach making a *cheshbon tzedek*.[179] The following is a free translation of a portion of the *sichah*, followed by a summary.

Although there is a principle that one can assume that every Jew is good and proper, this is limited to how one should view others; with regard to oneself one cannot rely on this assumption.[180] Rather, he must periodically examine his spiritual status through conducting a *cheshbon tzedek* of all of his thoughts, words, and actions. He should then resolve to fix and complete whatever is needed, and more important—he should actually fix and complete them. . . .

When a person makes a *cheshbon tzedek*, he is primarily focused on how to actually improve the details of his conduct, one detail at a time. Because of this, he may feel limited to these details and lack excitement and enthusiasm. It is therefore important to also adopt another approach to *teshuvah*, so that he will feel excited and accomplished.

---

178. *Sefer Hasichos* 5752, Vol. 1, pp. 62–64.
179. Lit., an honest account (of oneself). In general, this term is synonymous with the term *cheshbon hanefesh*, an accounting of one's soul.
180. See *Pirkei Avos*, Chapter 2, Mishna 4: "Do not trust yourself until the day you die."

[The Rebbe will explain another approach to teshuvah and why both are needed:]

Instead of focusing on all of the details that need improvement, he should elevate himself to a higher level where he is completely focused on learning Torah, davening, and other spiritual matters, and as a result, all of his previous problems will automatically disappear. Just like a small amount of light dispels a large amount of darkness, the light of his increased involvement and excitement in spirituality will automatically dispel the negative matters that must be fixed. The greater his involvement and excitement in positive matters, the more the negative matters will fade away.

The problem with this approach is that one isn't focused on correcting all of the details of his conduct, since he is concentrating on increasing in learning Torah and other positive things.

The true and best way is to adopt a combination of these two approaches. One should make a detailed *cheshbon tzedek* of all of his thoughts, words, and actions, and he should infuse into this *cheshbon tzedek* a recognition that through these detailed actions he will be elevated to a completely higher level. In other words, he feels within each detail that requires improvement how this brings him closer to the higher and more exciting level of closeness to Hashem he is striving to reach. (This is in direct contrast to viewing it as a list of chores weighing him down. Instead, each detail is seen as an essential component to fulfilling his desire to come close to Hashem in a much greater way.)[181] Through this, he will have the proper (and incomparably more) enthusiasm and excitement in his self-refinement.

Besides for the effectiveness in terms of actual improvement, there is an additional benefit to this combined approach.

When someone sees that there are many areas that need improvement, he might feel discouraged and become depressed. However, that will only happen if he is focusing on the magnitude of these negative areas. But if his focus lies on the idea that through correcting these aspects he will reach a deeper level of closeness to Hashem, he won't feel depressed at all; he will be joyful and excited that he is uniting with Hashem.

On a deeper level, not only does one become closer to Hashem through improving his conduct, but the entire purpose of his previous situation was to enable him to connect more deeply to Hashem through *teshuvah*.

When a Yid does *teshuvah*, he fully reveals his deepest connection to Hashem. This is expressed by the burning desire to come close to Hashem that wells up within him despite his low level, demonstrating that his connection to Hashem is beyond any limitations, even the limitations of his spiritual

---

181. The following incident was printed in the weekly *Here's My Story* publication (Tishrei or Cheshvan 5775):

Someone once asked the Rebbe, "Why does Hashem want us to be careful with so many minute details, for example, to have separate spoons for meat and milk?"

"It's not for Him, it's for us," the Rebbe answered. "This is the path Hashem gave us through which we can become close to Him."

In other words, all the details each one of us must work on are the path Hashem lovingly gave us to come closer to Him.

shortcomings. The revelation of this deep connection is so significant that Hashem allows negative things to happen so that a person will achieve this revelation. Thus, a Yid can feel that the only reason there are details that need improvement to begin with is to reveal the depth of connection experienced through *teshuvah*.

By considering these two ideas (first, how every detail will bring him to a completely higher level of closeness to Hashem, and second, how these aspects are only there to bring him to the deepest experience of *teshuvah*), a person will be able to work on fixing these areas with great happiness and enjoyment.

In summary, there are two classic approaches to *teshuvah*:[182]

1. To examine every detail of your thoughts, speech, and actions and make a detailed plan of how to fix whatever needs correction.
2. To devote yourself completely to learning and *davening*, thereby elevating yourself to a higher level. When you are in such a position, you won't want to be involved in the wrong things to begin with.

Each of these approaches has an advantage and a disadvantage, as follows:

1. In the first approach, one is actually focused on fixing all the aspects that need improvement. However, since he is completely caught up in the details and is only thinking about how to accomplish what must get

---

182. See *Hayom Yom*, 28 Menachem Av, where these two approaches are brought and explained.

done, his excitement is very limited.[183] In addition, since he notices that he has many faults that need improvement, he might become sad or depressed about his situation.

2. The advantage of the second approach is that one is excited and lively about everything he does and has a positive frame of mind. The problem is that since he isn't focusing on the details that need correction, he can't completely fix them.

The Rebbe explains that the correct path is to combine these two approaches. You should narrow in on all the details that need improvement, but then infuse into your plan of improvement the awareness that each detail is imperative for you to reach a higher level of closeness to Hashem. In other words, you should realize that the way to become completely absorbed into a higher level of reality is not only by focusing on learning and davening, but also through working on the details of your conduct that need improvement. Each small detail is not merely a detail for itself but part of something tremendous—the ability to come closer to Hashem on a whole new level.

When you begin to look at it this way, you won't feel limited by the things you have to work on; instead, you will feel free to fulfill the yearning of your *neshamah* to come closer to Hashem by working on yourself. Additionally, you won't have any reason to feel despondent, since rather than looking at them as problems, you will view them as opportunities for infinite growth and closeness to Hashem.[184]

---

183. This is similar to the general problem of a person who is very meticulous to keep all the details of Halacha but is lacking the inner spirit behind his actions, causing them to be done with a cold exactness.
184. Someone once complained to the Rebbe that his doctor told him he had a certain illness and needs to take medicine to cure it, and this piece of news had lowered

On a deeper level, you should realize that the underlying reason there are areas that need improvement is to give you the great merit of *teshuvah*, enabling you to reach a level of closeness to Hashem even a tzaddik can't attain.

---

his spirits. The Rebbe explained to him that this was actually a reason to be happy. Beforehand, he hadn't been aware of his sickness; the fact that his doctor had showed him how to get better only improved his situation.

Similarly, discovering things that need improvement and planning to fix them is not a disheartening realization but a positive one.

Chapter 8.
THINKING CHASSIDUS BEFORE GOING TO SLEEP

The Baal Shem Tov explains that the first thought a person has in the morning affects his entire day.[185] Chassidim add that the same applies to the first words a person speaks and the first action he performs.[186] For this reason, the first words a person says are *Modeh Ani*, his first thought is that he is in the presence of Hashem, and his first action is to wash *negel vasser*.

This idea is likewise applicable to the final things a person does before going to bed. Therefore, the last action of a Yid is to place *negel vasser* at his bedside, his last words are to say *Hamapil*, and his final thoughts should be to think over an idea in Chassidus. These thoughts will affect the way you sleep so that it should be how Hashem wants, and they will make it easier for you to wake up energetically to serve Hashem.

This is different than the *cheshbon hanefesh* made by *Krias Shema Al Hamitah*. Then you are thinking about your personal growth, whereas here you are thinking about an idea in Chassidus, not necessarily how it pertains to your *avodah*. This should be done (before or) after *Hamapil* and immediately before sleeping, not during *Krias Shema Al Hamitah*.

---

185. כתר שם טוב סי' ריב.
186. I heard this from R. Aryeh Leib Kaplan, *Rosh Yeshiva* in Montreal, who heard it from R. Shlomo Chaim Kesselman.

The Frierdiker Rebbe says[187] that the time after *Hamapil* should be spent thinking over words of Torah. Some chassidim mention that a person should think over Tanya,[188] but you can review any idea in Chassidus, as long as it keeps your mind fully occupied.[189] The Rebbe writes in Hayom Yom[190] that when a person's mind is not engaged in thinking holy thoughts, it will automatically be open to accepting unholy ones. The only way to have proper thoughts before going to sleep is by thinking holy thoughts, especially ideas of Chassidus.

Going to sleep is a very special time; it is the time you are preparing your *neshamah* to go up and receive a renewed dose of life and energy from Hashem. You should try to put yourself in the proper frame of mind so that your *neshamah* will receive vitality from the *tzad hakedushah* and you will be able to wake up with renewed energy and vigor, prepared to use the day in its fullest to serve Hashem.

---

187. סה"ש תש"א ע' 56.
188. I heard this from R. Pinye Korf. See also *Reb Shlomo Chaim* (pp. 290 and 572) where he speaks about thinking over a *perek Tanya* before *Krias Shema Al Hamitah*.
189. A related idea is the following *eitzah* I once heard from R. Menachem Zev Halevi Greenglass *a"h:* To help a person sleep properly, he should repeat the names of the *Rebbeim* before *Hamapil* (starting with the Rashbi and the Arizal and then continuing with the Baal Shem Tov), including their names and their mothers' names.
190. ט"ז חשון.

לע"נ

מרים בת **צבי הירשל**

נפטרה כח' תמוז תשע"ה

נדבת **משפחתברודנו**

לע"נ

מרת **רבקה יהודית** בת ר' **אשר אנשיל**

נפטרה כ' סיון ה'תשס"ט

ומרת **מרים** בת ר' **משה**

נפטרה ה' תשרי ה'תשס"ו

נדבת **משפחת ליבליך**

לזכות שמחת הנישואין של
החתן הת' **מנחם מענדל** שיחי'
וב"ג הכלה **אסתר** שתחי'

ליום יז' אדר ב' שנת הקהל תשע"ו

נדבת ההורים **ארי' לייב ולאה**
חוטארעצקי

לזכות

רחל לאה בת **הינדא שרה** לרפו"ש וקרובה

החייל בצבאות ה' **ישראל אריה לייב** בן **חיה מושקא**

לע"נ

חי' איטא בת **חנה לאה**

ר' **מרדכי אברהם** בן **חי' איטא**

הת' **אורי ניסן** בן הר' **מנחם מענדל**

לז"נ

ר' **דובער** ב"ר **גרשון** ע"ה נפטר כ"ט תשרי תשנ"ז

ורעיתו מ' **יאשא ליבא** ב"ר **דוד** ע"ה נפטרה י"ט ניסן תשנ"ט

ת' נ' צ' ב' ה'

לע"נ

הרב **יצחק אייזיק** בן הרב **משה** ע"ה

נפטר ט"ז טבת תשכ"ד

וזו' **מרת רחל** בת ר' **אברהם** ע"ה

נפטרה ה' אלול תש"ד

ר' **אריה לייביש** בן ר' **אליקום געצל** הלוי ע"ה

נפטר ער"ח אלול תרע"ט

וזו' **מרת שרה** בת ר' **יעקב** הכהן ע"ה

נפטרה י' אב תשל"ה

לזכות הרה"ת **דובער** בן **שולמית** וכל משפחתו

נדבת משפחת נעש שיחיו

לזכות חיזוק ההתקשרות

לכ"ק אדמו"ר נשיא דורנו

הרעיא מהימנא הממשיך דעת באלקות לכל אנשי הדור

שנזכה לראות בקרוב ממש

ויוציאנו מהגלות הפנימי והגלות הגשמי

אל הגאולה האמיתית והשלימה

www.ingramcontent.com/pod-product-compliance
Lightning Source LLC
Chambersburg PA
CBHW061604110426
42742CB00039B/2773